Called to
Counsel

Called to Counsel

Dr. Timothy Foster

OLIVER
NELSON

A Division of Thomas Nelson Publishers
Nashville • Atlanta • Camden • New York

Published in Nashville, Tennessee, by Oliver-Nelson Books, a division of Thomas Nelson, Inc., Publishers, and distributed in Canada by Lawson Falle, Ltd., Cambridge, Ontario.

Scripture quotations are from the NEW KING JAMES VERSION. Copyright ©1979, 1980, 1982, Thomas Nelson, Inc., Publishers.

Unless specifically identified as factual, all names and events have been fictionalized for protection of privacy.

Printed in the United States of America.

Library of Congress Cataloging-in-Publication Data

Foster, Timothy.
  Called to counsel.

  1. Counseling. I. Title.
BF637.C6F57   1986   253.5   85-29790
ISBN 0-8407-9538-6 (pbk.)

Contents

Acknowledgments

Acknowledgments

I wish to gratefully acknowledge the support of my wife, Donna, and daughters, Tanya and Tara. Also, special thanks to Dr. John Hower, Omar Zook, and Robert M. Taylor for allowing me to share some of their ideas and creations with you.

And many thanks to the counselees, students, and teachers who have taught me far more than I have taught them.

CHAPTER

1

Getting Started

What does it mean to be called to counsel? Who is called? What good is a book on it?

This book is designed to give specific training and guidance to the Christian worker (professional or volunteer) involved in establishing and maintaining an effective counseling ministry. The ministry may be that of a Sunday school superintendent counseling with one of his teachers, an elder or a discipler with a member of the church, a campus worker with a student, pastors and pastors' wives with parishioners, or youth workers with youth. Loving Christians who want to show warmth and offer support to the people around them may also undertake such a ministry. In other words, the advice here is for virtually every concerned Christian who hasn't already had extensive counselor training.

I have made a conscious effort to make this book as practical and specific as possible. Instead of devoting space to the theories and philosophies of counseling, I have focused on the "what to do" and "what to say" guidelines and suggestions. I hope that you will want to keep this book handy as a reference and turn to it for ideas and suggestions from time to time.

In counseling, as in other areas of life, meaning well doesn't always mean doing well. People can have the best motivation in the world, but if they don't understand anything about the human mind or emotions, about basic counseling techniques,

1

good motivation may not be translated into actual helping behaviors. A well-motivated but psychologically naive person can actually make things worse.

Let me give you a good example. A young mother came to me in obvious distress. She was frightened and overwhelmed by guilt. Tearfully, she told me she was afraid she had not been sincere, years ago, when she asked Christ into her heart and life. She had been feeling this way for three weeks. The day before our appointment she had gone to talk to her pastor, and he picked up a Bible, pointed to it, and said, "All the help you need is in here. If you would just believe everything in this book, you wouldn't be depressed." As you might guess, she left the pastor feeling more guilty, more fearful, and more depressed.

I don't doubt the sincere motivation of that pastor for a minute, but if he had had any notion about what was wrong with that woman and how to help her, he wouldn't have resorted to the "it's in the Bible, believe it" approach. Most people want to help, but they get frustrated because they don't know how. Then they become impatient and say something like, "Now just pull yourself together and snap out of it." That is exactly what this young woman's mother told her after she left the pastor's office. Obviously, to avoid making a bad situation worse, potential counselors need to learn some basic counseling techniques.

What Is Counseling?

The answer to the question, what is counseling? is both simple and complex. The simple answer is that counseling is demonstrating Christ's understanding, love, and guidance to those in distress. Did you ever notice that two of Christ's most prominent titles relate directly to the ministry of counseling? In Isaiah 9:6 Christ is called both "Wonderful Counselor" and "Prince of

Peace." Also, Christ described the Holy Spirit as the "Comforter" or the "Helper." Since we are to be ambassadors and representatives of our Lord, we cannot be His adequate disciples if we have no idea how to counsel people toward a position and experience of peace. The counseling ministry is an integral part of what it means to be a servant of God and a Christian.

I deal with the complex answer throughout this book. There is, of course, much more to be said about Christian counseling than can be contained in any book, but I believe I can give you a good, basic understanding of what it is.

How Are You Really?

If a believer intends to be a comforter, a counselor, and an instrument of God's peace, the first issue each of us confronts is how to get started. We get started by noticing people, by really looking at them and listening to them, and then by letting them know that their condition matters to us. Some members of the Christian church, unfortunately, do not encourage others' openness and self-revelation.

Some years ago I was in an adult Sunday school class, and some topic of Christian behavior was being discussed. A woman in the class interrupted the discussion and said, "You know, I have been having a lot of trouble with this very issue this week. I wonder if the class would pray for me." I was impressed by this woman's bravery and lack of pretense. I found her later in church so I could tell her so. When I did, she said, "Oh, thank you. One of the women who was in the class already came up to me and said she thought I was out of line by asking for personal prayer in a Sunday school class. She didn't think it was the right time or place."

Most people, whether in churches or out, have learned to keep self-revelation to a minimum, because they have found out that most people really don't care about their pain. It seems that people are wrapped up in their own lives and don't even notice, let alone care, about the pain others experience.

If you are going to begin a counseling ministry in your class or your neighborhood, with your friends, at work, or in church, the first obstacle you have to overcome is people's learned reluctance to talk about themselves or to tell you how they really are. If you need proof that this is a problem in your society, think of how many times in the last week someone (perhaps even a total stranger) said to you, "Hi, how are you?" or "How is it going?" or "How are you doing?" Did you even once give a straight answer to these questions? Of course not. You said, "Fine," no matter how you were feeling. In our society, this is such a learned reflex that it is amazing how miserable we can feel and still come up with that positive response.

About a year ago, I received a call at church just before services were to start. My only sister was in real physical danger in the delivery of her first child. At that time, the heartbeats of both mother and son were weakening. I became quite upset. (They are both doing well now.)

I tried to tell some friends about it in the lobby, and I got teary just talking about it. Deciding I needed to be alone for a while, I headed out the door for the parking lot and my car. I passed several families on the way in to church. About half of them said, "Hi, how are you?" Can you guess what I said in reply? "Fine."

It's incredible isn't it? A man can be so upset he gets choked up and heads for his car, and he still says, "I'm fine." This tendency for the prospective counselee (the one who is upset) to answer "I am fine," regardless of how awful he may really feel, is the first hurdle the prospective counselor must overcome if any counseling is going to take place. You must remember that in our culture the greeting, "How are you?" is just that. It is a greeting and not really a question at all.

Partly because of that, and partly because of other social and cultural pressures to keep emotional expressions under control and weaknesses hidden, it is not easy for others to tell you how they really feel, even when you ask.

If you want to know how someone is, physically, spiritually, or emotionally, you will have to let that person know that your question is a genuine inquiry.

You can convey your interest with your body language, your tone of voice, the time and place of your question, and your follow-through. Obviously, asking "How are you?" as you pass someone in a hallway conveys a totally different message than when you stop in front of someone and say, "Bob, I have been thinking about you. How are you feeling?" and then wait for an answer. Even then, Bob may give an automatic "fine," but your follow-through question, "No, I mean how are you really?" will usually produce a more open response.

Sometimes well-meaning people miss out on the opportunity of the ministry of counseling by not noticing the setting or the social environment. You cannot expect a really open answer when the person you address is surrounded by people or on the way to a meeting or an activity. If you really want to know how someone is, you need to ask in a setting and time that permit you a genuine answer. This is often not easy to accomplish, particularly at church when time is limited and extended private conversations are difficult to accomplish.

The "how are you really?" approach is usually necessary to get things started. Most people who are really hurting will respond to genuine concern. Once the individual responds, continue to be aware of time and setting. If necessary, suggest going somewhere else. "Let's go outside and talk" or "Have you got a minute? Let's sit down. I'd like to hear more about this." You might want to suggest a time and place where you can get together and talk about it some more. If at all possible, agree on an appointment time right then. "Let's get together for breakfast on Thursday at 7:00," or, "I'll call you this afternoon to set up a time to get together"). Be absolutely sure if you make a commitment to meet someone at a certain time or to call that you follow through. If a counselor loses credibility, the ability to function as a counselor is lost.

As the helper or the counselor, you have the initial responsibility to let people know that you are genuinely interested and to make it possible for them to share with you if they want. If you have followed up with one or two questions, the setting has been right, and they still don't share with you, that is certainly their right. Don't try to force the issue. Later they may remember your helping attitude toward them and may turn to you for counsel.

What People Need Most

We turn now to the counselor's focus and the counselee's need. What most people need when they are upset can be summarized in two words, *understanding* and *caring*. If your dog eats the rest of this book before you get to finish it, your reading thus far will not have been a total loss if you remember and apply these two words.

To the counselee, *understanding* means that you (the counselor) have heard what has been said, and that you have some idea of what he must be feeling. You can communicate your understanding (1) by listening and (2) by telling the counselee what you think he is feeling: "That must have been awful," "I'll bet that made you angry," "Ouch! That must have hurt," or "He must have meant a lot to you."

You will notice that these examples are each only one sentence long. This is not by accident. One of the biggest mistakes novice or untrained counselors make is talking too much. Try to keep your comments limited to one sentence at a time, two at the most. If the counselee disagrees with your statement by saying something like, "No, I didn't feel angry, I felt disappointed," don't argue, even though you may be right. Arguing someone into agreement is not counseling, and it is not going to help the situation. Understanding means you, the counselor, are to understand the counselee, not the other way around.

Let's assume that a wife is upset, which puts the husband in the counseling role. Here is an example of some understanding responses.

Linda came home from the store in tears. "I'll never go back there again. I could have just died."

"What happened?" asked Fred.

"I wrote a check to pay for the children's clothes. When the salesclerk saw my name on the check she called the manager. My name was on a list of people who had written bad checks. The manager came out, and all these people were standing in line while he told me I had written two bad checks in there before. Then I said, 'No way was that me,' and I started to cry. Finally he took me to his office to show me the checks. They were written by some woman with the same name as mine, but she had a different middle name and an E in her last name. Then the manager was really apologetic, but we were in his office and nobody heard him apologize to me. After that, he went out and yelled at the cashier. I'm never going back there!"

How do you respond to meet her needs in that situation?

a. Say it was just a mistake. It could happen to anybody. Don't worry about it.
b. Get mad and go see the manager.
c. Call a lawyer.
d. Tell her what she should have done.
e. Tell her God had a purpose in it.
f. None of the above.

The answer is (f) None of the above. More than anything she wants your understanding, and none of these statements communicates understanding to her. Here are some possible responses.

a. Oh! That must have been awful.
b. You must have felt like going through the floor.
c. I'll bet you felt like punching somebody.

Any of these responses would have been good. Notice in each of them the speaker is telling what he thinks she was feeling. That communicates understanding.

The second thing for the counselor to communicate is *caring*. This is not as easy to define. I think it is mostly communicating an attitude that says the counselee matters to you. You show an interest in what the counselee has been going through or what he is feeling. Saying, "I care," is probably the poorest way to communicate caring. Nodding, listening, speaking with a gentle tone of voice, and expressing genuine concern communicate caring. Listening to the counselee's story rather than telling yours shows love.

Caring is communicated by "I" messages. Statements such as "I am sorry that happened," "I don't blame you," or "I wish people wouldn't treat you that way" all communicate caring. Primarily though, caring is communicated by an attitude. Focusing all your attention on someone and really listening are clear signs of caring. You must let the person know that what is said matters to you. Respond the way you would like people to respond to you.

Let's use the same example with the wife who is upset. Adding your own feelings to your statements about her feelings will add depth and warmth to your responses.

a. Oh! That must have been awful. I am so sorry that happened.
b. You must have felt like going through the floor. I wish I could have been there with you.

c. I'll bet you felt like punching somebody. I certainly don't blame you.

When you don't know what to say, a simple caring response, such as, "Oh, I am so sorry," by itself is not at all bad.

If you tell your counselee how you feel about his or her feelings, only do so when what you feel is positive. If you think that what the counselee feels is inappropriate, don't say that. In those cases just stick to saying what you think the individual is feeling.

Don't Fix It

These suggestions about focusing on understanding and caring will help the counselor avoid making the biggest mistake made by novice counselors. What is the mistake? Trying to "fix" the problem of the counselee. I know that this statement is emotionally hard to take for a lot of readers. Someone is probably thinking, *What do you mean, I'm not supposed to fix the problem? What good is counseling if I don't help people?*

Counselors do help people, but not by telling them what they should do. Certainly many counselees will ask you, "What should I do?" Even if you think you know what they should do, you are almost certainly wasting your breath if you tell them. The key word is *tell.* A counselor almost never tells. Guiding counselees toward discovering a direction or a course of action is often appropriate, but "fixing," "advice giving" or "telling" are almost never appropriate counselor goals or responses.

Why is this so? Because no matter what they tell you, people don't want your advice, they rarely need it, and they almost never listen to it. If they do follow your advice, they frequently do so in order to blame you when things go wrong. I wish I didn't sound so cynical, but believe me, my attitude is far from cynical. Even if people "want" you to be responsible for them, what they "need" is to be responsible for themselves. I think people instinctively know that they are held responsible for their own behavior and need to make their own decisions, but many people don't want to admit this. It is so much easier to have someone else make decisions for them.

The counselor's role, then, is not so much fixing as it is doing other things: helping the counselees see what they are doing or not doing; clarifying their alternatives and the consequences of various alternatives; pointing out what they are avoiding; reminding them of what they believe and know to be true; and suggesting activities that help the counselees obtain a more accurate perception of themselves. All this is in addition to the main responsibilities of the counselor, which are understanding and caring. It may seem to you at this point that there is a lot to remember in effective counseling, but I believe my explanations in this book can make the process less mysterious and give hope to both counselor and counselee alike.

Before moving on, let's look at an example of caring and understanding without attempting to fix the problem.

BERT [*counselee*]. I appreciate this chance to talk to you, Dave. Frankly, I need some advice.

DAVE [*Bert's Sunday school teacher, friend and, in this example, counselor*]. Oh?

BERT. You know Cheryl started back to school this fall to finish her degree and the household seems to be really falling apart. The house is a mess. I never get an ironed shirt unless I iron it. At least three nights a week I end up baby-sitting with the kids. We never seem to have any time together. She seems happier, but the kids and I aren't happy at all. I am considering having her quit school, at least until the kids are older. What do you think I should do?

Here you can see Bert's statement of the problem as he sees it and his explicit request for advice. Notice now how much more helpful it is to Bert when Dave does not tell him what to do but rather offers understanding, caring, and guidance.

DAVE. Sounds like you have had a rough couple of months.

BERT. That is for sure. I never figured it would be this bad.

DAVE. It sounds kind of annoying.

BERT. Yes, it is, but it is also lonely. I have begun to feel like a single parent.

DAVE. That sounds like a bad feeling.

BERT. You're telling me.

DAVE. Have you talked with Cheryl yet about how you feel?

BERT. No, not yet. I was trying to decide first what to do and then tell her.

DAVE. So you could tell her what you decided?

BERT. Yes.

DAVE. Do you always decide what you are going to do before you have shared your feelings with Cheryl or listened to hers?

BERT. It does sound like that is what I am doing, doesn't it?

DAVE. Yes.

BERT. You know, she has complained about my going off half-cocked before, but I always thought she was talking about my temper.

DAVE. What do you think she was trying to say?

BERT. That she doesn't like it when I overreact to something without listening to others first.

DAVE. Maybe you felt like deciding to do something was safer than just telling her what you felt.

BERT. I think I do that a lot.

DAVE. I wonder how she would feel if you told her about your discovery that you sometimes "react" or "tell" before sharing your own feelings or listening to what other people have to say?

BERT. She would probably be glad.

11

DAVE. It sounds like you are saying that the problem isn't so much what you should "tell her" you have decided. It sounds more like you need to share with her about your lonely feelings and see what the two of you can plan together to help that.

BERT. Yes, I know she would respond well to that.

Later on, I will discuss many of the specific counseling techniques used in this example, but you will notice how the real problem was faced through a combination of understanding, caring, and some gentle guidance. The question of "What should I do?" was never answered, but Bert got some real help.

Privacy and Confidentiality

Privacy and confidentiality are basic to successful counseling. You simply cannot and will not have an effective counseling ministry if you are not willing to commit yourself to every counselee's rights in these areas. The only exceptions to these rules will be covered in a later chapter, but these exceptions will rarely come up for most Christian counselors.

I knew of a pastor who frequently used situations from his counseling as illustrations in his sermons. He never understood why he had so few people coming to him for counseling. Once word gets out that you are not strict in the "keeping your mouth shut" category, your counseling days are virtually over. (By the way, the confidentiality issue is why I don't use the names or cases of any actual patients in my writing. Illustrations I use are fictitious. I believe to do otherwise would be wrong.)

The Setting

A few words about where to do counseling are in order in this chapter. A lot of helpful informal counseling takes place over a cup of coffee or a soft drink in a neighborhood family restaurant. The setting is a natural one, and the counselee will feel less self-conscious. The restaurant setting also avoids the potential embarrassment of trying to find a quiet place in a house full of people or the awkwardness of trying to keep children out of the living room and explaining why.

Pastors will be able to use the pastor's study for counseling, and other Christian workers have offices as well. When possible, your office is preferable to your home for counseling sessions. Frankly, it may be difficult sometimes to get people to leave after the counseling is over. When you are in your own home, you can't leave. Many people have an entire evening or afternoon taken up with what was really just a half-hour of counseling. It is important to think about your own family and to protect your time with them by not devoting four hours to a half-hour project. Other possible neutral settings include a park, the church, or a sports outing (golf, racket ball, tennis). Taking a counselee/friend along with you on an errand that will give you at least a half-hour of uninterrupted conversation can be a very useful way of being able to both talk and listen.

Protection

Many, many affairs have begun with men counseling women and vice versa. Unless you are in the full-time ministry and simply have no alternative, I urge you not to counsel members of the opposite sex. If and when it is absolutely necessary (and it is not necessary if you are a volunteer), you need to protect yourself. You can do this in several ways. You can have your own spouse counsel with you. Or you can have your spouse or a friend of the counselee wait in an adjoining room. Only see people of the opposite sex at appointment times and at designated places with appropriate safeguards. I know some folks may be surprised by my position, but I have seen so many tragedies, broken homes and broken churches, which could have been prevented by the counselors' being cautious, that I felt I needed to issue a warning.

Before we move on, I would like to end this chapter with a word of encouragement. You don't have to memorize every word of this book or any other to care for people. This book offers several ideas and techniques for your consideration, but the most important counseling tool is *you*.

2

The Counselor

A pianist has a piano, a surgeon a scalpel, and a plumber a wrench, but as a counselor, *you* are your primary tool. Just as a violinist cannot perform at the ultimate best if the violin is out of tune, so you must be in tune with yourself and God to be the best counselor you can be. Who you are as a person, what you are, and what you believe make all the difference in the world as to what kind of counseling you do. Effective counseling cannot be separated from the effective counselor.

This chapter will focus on you as a person and how you affect the counseling process. We will look at your spiritual position. And we will consider the counselor's role as prophet and priest.

What Is Your Source?

Perhaps the most important part of who you are as a counselor is your source of strength or power. On whom or what do you depend to do effective counseling? Some people depend on their own intuition or on what they call "common sense"; others expect God to lead them; and still others depend on their mastery of counseling and an understanding of psychology. Is one of these more important than the other?

Although many psychologists and other professionals in the field of psychotherapy and counseling agree that there is often an element of art in therapy, one of the main reasons professional counselors go to school is because we believe in the science of psychology and the rational, scientific study of psychotherapy. It is not surprising, therefore, that professionals become a bit cautious at the mention of the use of faith in counseling.

Faith sounds very much like the excuse a novice counselor might give to a supervisor when asked: "Why did you suddenly switch to a different technique in the middle of a session?"

"Well," the student might answer, "I did it on faith."

Many of us remember the classic biblical definition of faith: "Faith is the substance of things hoped for, the evidence of things not seen" (Heb. 11:1). Something hoped for doesn't sound very scientific, does it? Yet faith plays an important part in counseling.

Faith in Counseling

Similar to the way in which we all have faith in the chairs on which we sit, and faith in the unseen air we breathe, faith is a part of our lives regardless of our specific religious affiliation. We all actively depend on things we cannot immediately verify, such as whether a bottle with a label for a particular medication does, in fact, contain that medication or whether the articles in professional journals are based on real rather than bogus studies. Therefore, I will define *faith* as "active dependence." For our purposes, I will discuss the counselor's active dependence on God.

Should counselors depend on God in the process of counseling? The answer to this question may seem obvious, but to some the answer is an obvious yes while to others, who think it is an unscientific approach, the answer is an obvious no. What does the Bible say? Turn to the gospel of John 15:1–9, which sets forth an analogy Jesus gave to demonstrate dependence on God. Jesus said,

"I am the true vine, and My Father is the vinedresser. Every branch in me that does not bear fruit He takes away; and every branch that bears fruit He prunes, that it may bear more fruit....Abide in Me, and I in you. As the branch cannot bear fruit of itself, unless it abides in the vine, neither can you, unless you abide in Me. I am the vine, you are the branches, He who abides in Me, and I in him, bears much fruit; for without Me you can do nothing....If you abide in Me, and My words abide in you, you will ask what you desire, and it shall be done for you. By this My Father is glorified, that you bear much fruit; so you will be My disciples. As the Father loved Me, I also have loved you; abide in My love."

We have here a clear, powerful statement that dependence upon God through faith is essential if we are to bear fruit. This fruit, of course, is the fruit of the Spirit, which begins with love and includes joy, peace, patience, sensitivity, and self-control (see Gal. 5:22–23). Who will deny that our counseling would be more effective if we had a limitless and sure source of love, patience, sensitivity, and so on?

To further study the appropriateness of the counselor's active dependence upon God, let's examine briefly what the Bible has to say about the opposite of active dependence, namely, self-sufficiency.

Self-Sufficiency

When we go to God's Word to discover His goals for us, we find that His goals are very different from society's goals. Society teaches and rewards self-sufficiency. I received a grade on my report card every six weeks or so from the time I was in elementary school in the category of "Independence and Self-Reliance."

Throughout the Bible we see, in contrast, God hates self-sufficiency. The following verses give examples of this: "Because you have trusted in your works and your treasures, / You shall be taken" (Jer. 48:7); "If anyone thinks that he knows anything, he knows nothing yet as he ought to know" (1 Cor. 8:2); "If anyone among you seems to be wise in this age, let him become a fool that he may become wise" (1 Cor. 3:18); and "Not that we are sufficient of ourselves to think of anything as being from ourselves, but our sufficiency is from God" (2 Cor. 3:5).

Throughout God's Word we see that Satan's basic sin is trying to usurp God's throne and to be God himself. Humankind's most basic sin is different in quality from that. Most people really don't seem to care if God is in the universe as long as He doesn't bother them. Thus, the basic sin is ignoring God, not rebelling against Him. It is as though people were saying, "That's fine, you be God, rule the universe, decide when tornadoes occur and where lightning strikes. Meanwhile, I am going to go my own way with my own life, do my own work in my own style, and ignore you as much as possible."

It is very much a part of our human nature to be functional atheists. We function (yes, even believers) as though God is not intimately involved in our lives and our activities. We may claim to be supernaturalists (that is, believing that God is involved in our lives), but many of our activities and expectations are naturalist or scientific (that is, believing there is a purely rational, predictable, and repeatable cause and effect for everything).

I believe that God is intimately involved in our daily lives and our ministries. As I noted earlier, the names of Christ include Wonderful Counselor and Prince of Peace. I think that means that Christ himself is intimately involved in our counseling and that, in fact, much of what we do in counseling is representing Him. He wants to work through us to tend His sheep.

Elements of Dependency

Now let's discuss what is involved in dependence on God in the counseling process. I can summarize this with two key words: *acknowledgment* and *action*.

First, we must acknowledge our own limitations and therefore our need for God to be the source of our ongoing work. In other words, as branches, we must acknowledge that we cannot bear fruit of ourselves and acknowledge that we must be, as it were, "plugged" into the vine in order to bear fruit.

I would like to recommend some specific suggestions here for keeping our dependence where it needs to be. We should offer frequent silent prayers, seeking God's direction in our counseling and seeking His work in the lives of our counselees. This includes praying for ourselves to be sensitive, loving, and caring and for our counselees to be healed or to grow, whether the healing and growth come as a result of their relationship with us, from their reading a book, or from any of the possible sources of insight.

God is the source of healing. It really doesn't matter whether He chooses to heal a person through us nearly so much as it matters that He heals that person. We must not be offended if God chooses to help someone through some means other than ourselves. God doesn't need our ability; He wants our availability.

To be available we need to be in tune and responsive, like any good instrument. We stay in tune by reading His Word, talking to Him, talking about Him, and checking our tuning regularly. Violins can get out of tune in a matter of a few minutes, all by themselves. Christians have an even worse problem because we have an old nature constantly pulling at us. Just because we were in tune yesterday doesn't mean we are in tune today.

We should avoid all actions that tend to get us out of tune. I won't insult you by listing these for you. How could I know what gets you out of tune? I suggest, however, that sometimes the question of whether a behavior is right or wrong, sin or not sin in and of itself, may not be as important a question as whether it will keep you in tune or pull you out of tune with God.

The second key word is *action*. I have suggested *active* dependence rather than passive dependence on God. If there is a weakness in suggesting that as Christian counselors we depend upon God, that weakness (or caution) is that we as counselors might sit back and passively wait for God to do something without our becoming involved or committed in the process. That is why I say that active dependence (or faith) is what is necessary for God to work through us. Active dependence perhaps can be illustrated by what I frequently experience in leading a psychodrama group (psychodrama is a form of group therapy). Someone on the other side of the room may begin to cry or in some way express an obvious need for support. At that point I am aware that this counselee has a need. I may be aware that love is required, but I may not feel the emotion of love for that person. Active dependence is neither praying that someone else express love nor is it waiting on my side of the circle until I feel an overwhelming love for the counselee. I quite literally need to take not one step of faith but perhaps a dozen as I walk around the circle, both praying and assuming that by the time I reach the person, God will have given me the love that the person needs. I have found that it works.

Benefits of Dependency

When we discuss the benefits of depending upon God in counseling, perhaps the most important and most obvious one is that God provides the limitless, sure source of unconditional acceptance, of patience, sensitivity, and many other attributes counselors need to be successful. In addition, depending on

God produces a sense of confidence. We know that God is willing to help, and if we are willing to depend upon Him, the only additional "will" that is needed for real growth to take place is the will of the counselee. The counselor's confidence gives the counselees confidence, and this, of course, makes it easier for the counselees to invest themselves in the counseling process.

Another benefit deals with the responsibility issue. If I know that in counseling someone I depended upon God and shared the best insights and the best love I could, then it relieves the sense of personal failure if the counseling fails to produce healing.

We all know that we are not perfect counselors. We all know that we do not have unconditional love for all of our counselees all of the time. Acknowledgment of that limitation is the first step toward being a channel for limitless love. If the counselee fails to accept it or if the counseling fails for some other reason, even though we will have personal feelings about that, we will have a much easier time in resolving our own sense of loss.

Christ addressed the issue of how to react when people don't respond well to you or your message. When Christ sent His disciples off to minister in His name (much as you counsel in His name), He said to them, "Whoever will not receive you nor hear you, when you depart from there, shake off the dust under your feet as a testimony against them" (Mark 6:11). I think the message here is that having fulfilled your responsibility, don't take the dirt with you. Don't carry with you the residue of someone else's unbelief. Shaking the dust off before you leave doesn't mean a verbal curse, but it does mean to leave the problem and go on to your next opportunity to minister.

Another benefit is that of modeling. When the counselee sees the counselor appropriately depending upon God, it is easier to be appropriately dependent on the counselor as well as on God.

One final benefit worth mentioning is success. Second Corinthians 2:14 says, "Now thanks be to God who always leads us in triumph in Christ." Depending on God produces counseling that usually helps people. Everyone may not want to change, but our being available for God gives us the opportunity to be used in the counseling process.

Competent without Training

This dependence on God might lead a person to reason that no training in the scientific method of communication, emotional dynamics, and counseling is necessary because all we have to do to be competent is depend upon God. But, I wonder, do we apply that reasoning to other fields? Do we apply that reasoning to becoming a surgeon? Do we say, "Don't go to medical school, trust God, and cut wherever the Spirit leads"? Of course not. Do we even use that method for making a chocolate cake? No. There is nothing ungodly about following a plan or getting some instruction in something that we want to learn how to do.

So we have not one truth here but two. On the one hand, it is appropriate and, I believe, godly to work on improving our technical skills and our understanding. We are told in Matthew 25 to invest and improve our talents. This is the scientific, rational, and natural part of counseling in psychology. But if, on the other hand, we attempt to do that counseling in our own strength, we have missed the supernatural part. While technically proficient counseling might help some people, it can't be truly powerful unless counselors are plugged into the supernatural energy source—the Spirit of God. We need the kind of dependence and connection illustrated by Jesus' story of the vine and the branches (see John 15:1-8). It is, therefore, our responsibility both to invest in improving our skills and to actively, consciously, and perhaps hourly depend on God's Spirit for His healing power, His fruit, and His direction.

The Counselor
Prophet or Priest?

As we look at the role of the Christian counselor, there are two separate functions or roles of a counselor which, though very different, are often confused. The two roles are both legitimate functions of members of the body of Christ, but one is much more appropriate for a counselor in most situations. The roles are prophet and priest.

We may think of the prophet in our culture as one who tells the future, but that is not the full meaning of the word *prophet*. A *prophet* is one who "tells forth." A pastor is often in the role of prophet when he is giving his Sunday morning message. He is preaching, proclaiming truth, lecturing, and talking to the congregation.

We often expect a pastor to know how to counsel, when in fact the skills necessary for his role of proclaimer of truth (prophet) are very different from the skills necessary for the role of a successful counselor. Although many pastors have learned both sets of skills, being proficient in one role is absolutely no guarantee of proficiency in another. In the same way, if we perceive the role of counselor as being one who lectures, confronts, and tells, we are not likely to do much listening as counselors. A misconception of the role is what is ultimately responsible for most unsuccessful counseling attempts. In fact, because most counseling is different from the prophetic "telling forth," some pastors end up being poor counselors. They do not understand the difference between their function in the pulpit and their function in the counseling room. When we try to preach to someone who is in pain, that person feels belittled, condemned, and misunderstood, not understood, comforted, and consoled. A pastor who is a successful counselor is successful for the same reasons that a nonpastor is a successful counselor. Successful counseling comes from understanding, caring, and guiding, in the power of the Holy Spirit.

The priestly function is much more in line with what is necessary for a successful counselor. The priestly role means that the counselor comforts rather than confronts, interviews rather than lectures, listens rather than preaches, and talks "with" rather than tells or talks "to." For the most part, the function of the Christian counselor is to comfort the disturbed, while the prophetic function is more likely to disturb the comfortable.

Guiding the Counselee to the Truth

In the context of an ongoing counseling relationship, there are occasional exceptions when the counselor may purposely shift gears and teach, preach, lecture, or confront for a moment. These are the exceptions, however, and not the rule. The rule is to guide the counselee to truth, not to give it.

If you are counseling with someone who is upset about how her roommate is constantly taking advantage of her, you might be tempted to say, "Get out of the situation." But that is telling rather than leading. Saying, "I wonder why you stay there?" is a better response because it leads the counselee to think about that question. Or you could say, "I guess you must be wondering why you continue to put up with that?" Leading questions like these should not be used early in a counseling session, but they might be very helpful toward the end of the session.

Look at two possible responses to a counselee. As a counselor, you might say, "Well, that's your whole problem. You have been sinning, and you have to stop." Or you might say, "I wonder if you felt that that is what Christ wanted you to do?" The second example leads the counselee to confront the situation. You can readily see that the approach of guiding rather than challenging or condemning would be better received and more helpful to a counselee.

A few weeks ago I talked to a Christian man who was having severe family problems because he was rarely at home and he was exhausted when he was there. He told me that he held two jobs. Although the family was not deeply in debt, he wanted the money for security. I asked him, "I wonder if you are aware that what you say you believe about Christ's supplying your needs and being your security does not seem to square with your putting the financial security of your family on the top of your priority list, even above your meeting the family's need to have you there?" That gentleman thought a lot about this on his own, and he made his own decision to quit one of his jobs and bring his behavior in line with his beliefs. I never told him to do it. I led him to a point where he could tell himself to do it. Even God Himself does not force us to do things. He invites, He knocks, He asks, He waits. I think we can do no less.

There is a big difference between being a chauffeur and being a driver education instructor. If you hired me to be your chauffeur, my main objective would be to move you from point A to point B. If I knew how to drive and you did not, it would certainly be more efficient for me to do the driving. If, on the other hand, you hired me to teach you to drive, then whether we are going from point A to B or from C to D is less important than whether I am teaching you how to make your own decisions and how to pilot your own vehicle. A counselor is not supposed to be a chauffeur, taking responsibility for getting people from point to point. A counselor is supposed to be an instructor, helping people learn how to take responsibility for themselves and how to determine which direction they will take.

3

The Counseling Process

A significant difference between Ford Motor Company and Disney World is that Ford manufactures products and Disney provides an experience. It is vital for the counselor to realize that the purpose of counseling is not so much the manufacturing of a cure as it is encouraging the experience of one.

Both novice and fully trained counselors often focus their attention on helping a counselee uncover some hidden memory, feeling, or belief that, when uncovered, will prove to be "it," something that will produce an immediate and permanent cure. But effective counseling focuses much more on the process than on a pot of gold at the end of the journey. Effective counseling is not dispensing truth nearly so much as it is helping the counselee discover the truth for himself and experience something on the way. Therefore, who you are as a person has everything to do with effective counseling, because effective counseling means being a counselor *with* someone, not *to* someone.

The Therapeutic Relationship

Another way of saying all of this is to say that effective counseling is not working for a trophy at the end. Effective counseling comes from the experience itself and, more specifically, from the relationship that develops between the counselor and the counselee. Believe it or not, what happens between the two of you in terms of relationship is far more important and more effective in helping the counselee than any little pearls of wisdom you might think of to say. The relationship itself has much more to do with the healing process than any answers that may be dispensed as part of the counseling. It is a little like a cruise to nowhere that is currently being advertised. People get on a ship, sail around in circles for a couple of days, and then return home. The destination isn't what the firm is selling, it is the experience of being on a cruise.

Counselor and counselee are on a trip together, and the quality of the ride ends up being more important to the goal of resolving the problem than the speed or even the direction taken.

You Are What You Imagine

Sometimes people get so caught up in negative experiences that they can no longer imagine what a positive experience would be like. They get so caught up in negative expectations that they can no longer imagine themselves doing well. Mental images work the other way too.

One of the things that made the 1984 United States Olympic Team so successful was the application of this truth through sports psychology. The athletes were taught to picture in their minds the way that they wanted to perform their skills. They imagined themselves jumping over the bar or spinning, twisting, and landing perfectly. This same, simple truth explains why in baseball, batters have slumps and streaks. It is a fact that if he cannot imagine himself hitting the ball out of the park, he cannot hit it out of the park.

As we attempt to build relationships or reach goals in life, we are controlled, propelled, and hampered by what we expect or by what we imagine will happen. Surely, sometimes we are surprised and things go better than we thought they would. And sometimes things go worse. But to a great extent, our behavior approaches (aims for) our mental images.

Some readers may be wondering why I have introduced the subject of mental imagery in a chapter about the counseling process. I mention it because the people you counsel have certain expectations about their relationship with you, based on their self-images and their history (or experiences) with other people. The therapy process is often healing (almost regardless of what you the counselor actually say) if you enable the counselees to imagine themselves well and in a safe, accepting, positive relationship, because they have experienced that kind of relationship with you.

Perhaps that is the hardest principle for the new counselor to grasp—that very often the relationship does the healing rather than the counselor's words of wisdom. But knowing this enables us to worry less about not having all the answers and to focus more on skills that really do help people feel better and actually be better.

Empathy

The first and most important skill to learn after realizing you must depend upon God is to be *empathic*. *Empathy* means "being able to participate in someone else's emotions and thoughts," that is, it is feeling and thinking like someone else, putting yourself in that person's place. (Empathy and sympathy are similar, but empathy implies a closer identification with another person, while sympathy implies more emotional distance.) It is amazing how many needs are met when someone empathizes with another person.

Ever since the Fall (see Gen. 2) when Adam and Eve rebelled, lost their innocence, and became alienated from God and from each other, humankind's basic needs—once met in their intimate fellowship with God—have not been met automatically. Notice how sin produced feelings of being unacceptable, exposed, and fearful: "Then the eyes of both of them were opened, and they knew they were naked" (Gen. 3:7). Adam told God, "I was afraid because I was naked" (Gen. 3:10).

In fact, Adam and Eve were no more naked after they ate the forbidden fruit than they were before. Their nakedness wasn't new. Before the Fall they felt perfectly comfortable with being completely open and exposed. The Fall did not make them naked. It made them feel unacceptable and afraid to reveal themselves.

God wants us to have the openness, trust, close relationship, peace, joy, and positive feelings about ourselves that humankind had before the Fall. Because we had those things and lost them, we still feel the need for them. If we can understand these basic human needs and empathize with those who come to us for counseling, we can help them experience something that gives them a taste of the "pre-Fall" openness, acceptance, and fellowship. In the counselor's relationship with the counselee, therefore, we should try to approximate (imperfect though it may be) the kind of interaction and fellowship that existed between God and Adam and Eve in the garden before the Fall.

How to Empathize

Knowing what you need to do and knowing how to do it are two different things, of course. Let's look at some good and bad examples of empathy.

I am writing this chapter while I am at a conference of Christian psychologists. This morning I went to a session that never quite got off the ground. A gentleman I will call Bob gave the presentation; he seemed ill at ease and never adequately developed his topic. As a result, there were very few questions after his presentation. He stopped a bit early, perhaps sensing that his audience was bored and restless. Suppose you are his friend, wife, or neighbor, and he will talk with you about his feelings when he arrives home tonight.

Bob says, "I really blew it this morning at that psychology

conference. I had to make that presentation. You know I had typed out the whole thing ahead of time so I would be organized, but I was afraid it would be boring to the people if I just read the whole thing, so I decided to just talk about what was in the paper.

"Well, I kept losing my train of thought. Then I would try to find where I was supposed to be in the paper. I would stop and look through the pages to find out what was next. There were long pauses. It was awful. I could sense the people getting restless. They started to look through their programs for what session to go to next. The more nervous I got, the worse I did. I know I must have looked like a jerk."

Before you read further, take a few seconds and come up with a statement that you might make to Bob if you were informally counseling with him after he made this statement.

Here are some examples of possible responses. Which ones communicate empathic understanding for Bob?

a. Well, I had to mow the grass this morning.

b. Yes, I screwed up like that once. I remember the boss asked me to give this report to the senior staff, and on the way to the meeting I dropped my folder. The pages got all out of order, and I didn't realize it until I started to give my report. I sure felt stupid.

c. I am sorry, Bob. That must have been awful.

d. That must be disappointing. I know you were hoping to increase your own confidence and your standing in that organization by giving a well-received paper.

e. Look, don't worry about it. We all screw up sometimes.

f. I am sure God was trying to teach you something.

Which of these answers do you think is the best? How about the worst? How did you decide? When you evaluate how empathic your responses are, notice whether you reflect exactly the same level of emotion as the counselee. Do you add a little understanding? Or does your response detract somewhat from the level of emotion in the problem statement? Occasionally, you may give a response that doesn't even indicate that you heard the person's problem. These are the things to look at when evaluating how empathic you have been.

Even though it may be obvious to many, I am going to take a minute to evaluate each of these possible statements. You may want to go back and do that yourself before reading how I rate them.

a. "Well, I had to mow the grass this morning." This is a very poor response. It gives no indication that the counselor has even heard Bob. How will Bob feel with a response like this? He will probably feel, *I must really be a boring person. Even my friend doesn't sound like he understands or hears me.*

b. "Yes, I screwed up like that once...." This is also a poor response. It is only slightly better than the first response. It does indicate that the counselor heard Bob, but the counselor focuses on himself and not on Bob. The counselor remembers his own past rather than tries to understand what Bob feels in the present.

c. "I am sorry, Bob. That must have been awful." This is an acceptable empathic response. Bob used the word *awful,* and the counselor has picked up on the same word. This does not add anything to Bob's understanding, but it does indicate to him that he has been heard and understood. If you were taking a counselor training course from me, I would say that this is the minimum level of empathic response I would accept. It is perfectly okay; there is nothing wrong with it. It just doesn't add anything. If a counselor can maintain this level of emotional interaction, the counselee will have some needs met and the relationship will grow.

d. "That must be disappointing...." This statement actually adds a dimension. Since Bob didn't use the word *disappointing*, this description of what Bob feels, with a word he didn't use, adds to his understanding of himself and his feeling that he is being cared for and understood. If your statement was like this one, you can give yourself an A.

e. "Look, don't worry about it...." I hope you didn't give this response a very high score. You will notice that it tells Bob what to do: "Don't worry." This is not an acceptable level of empathy. It may be well motivated, but it does not communicate much acceptance of Bob's emotional condition. This response tells Bob not to feel what he is feeling, and that is not a good counselor response.

f. "I am sure God was trying to teach you something." This is also a poor response that shows no empathy. While it may be true that God did have a purpose in the experience, counselors who are trying to show empathy, compassion, or loving-kindness need to avoid this kind of statement. Just using the word *God* doesn't make this an acceptable empathic response.

Guiding, Not Driving

Suppose your friend Bob is still upset about his poor presentation and continues to complain about it two months from now. Then you might wonder if it's okay to say, "God had a purpose in it," or even, "Grow up. No one wants to hear it anymore." Well, no, it isn't okay, although those sentiments might make sense after two months.

As I said earlier, there is a big teaching difference between teaching someone to drive a car and doing the driving yourself. The goal as counselor is to guide Bob to confront his own tendency to be upset about something after two months.

How should the counselor/friend respond to Bob? The counselor should guide to truth rather than give the truth. A statement such as, "I guess you must be wondering why this still bothers you so much after two months," would be good. Another possible statement would be, "I was wondering. Do things usually bother you for this long after something doesn't go the way you like?"

We want to help people learn to confront themselves. If a counselor says, "Can't you stop your whining and get on with your life?" the counselor might be accurate in the assessment of what Bob needs to do, but that kind of confrontation is rarely helpful.

If we as counselors try to convict other people, we try to do the job of the Holy Spirit. We are simply not equipped for that task. What happens is that people end up feeling condemned and judged rather than convicted. But if we can hold up a mirror and let people see themselves, if we can teach people to teach themselves, they can be led to confront their own sin or their own behavior.

I said earlier that the counseling role is similar to the priestly role. But counselors must be careful not to violate the priesthood of each counselee. Counselors should lead counselees to the point where they can do some of their own preaching to themselves. I refer to healthy "self-talk" here, not continual self-condemnation. When we help counselees look at the things they say to themselves, we help them with their internal guidance systems. This is obviously a lot healthier than having them depend on us to constantly tell them, "Turn left. Turn right. Do this. Do that."

A funny thing happens when we get caught up in driving for people instead of teaching them to drive. They become more and more passive and dependent on us but, at the same time, more and more angry. An axiom in psychology that is almost always true is: "Dependency produces anger." We need to be careful not to get caught up in the unhealthy relationships that occur when people "drive" other people.

Your job as counselor is to gently guide counselees through

the process of counseling and, within the context of your relationship, to help them see themselves and their emotions in a different light so that they can move on. Your understanding and caring make you an effective counselor.

4

Counseling Do's and Don'ts

How will I get them to talk?
How can I keep them talking?

These questions, often asked by novice counselors, have fairly easy answers. Most of the time, getting counselees started is hardly necessary because the people coming to you have already been thinking about what they want to say. Their difficulty has been finding someone to listen, understand, care, and keep quiet about it outside the counseling session.

If someone has asked to talk to you, all you really have to do to get that person started is to open the conversation. Often, you may begin with a sentence or two of small talk, especially if you are meeting someone and then going somewhere else for the session. You don't want to start counseling out in a hallway, so you can talk about the weather or whatever until you are both settled.

Once you are both seated and ready, however, it is time to get down to business. The counselor is the one responsible for shifting gears. If the counselee has asked to see you, just say something to direct attention to the problem.

Some good opening comments are, "Well, Bob, I know you had something you wanted to talk with me about. Why don't you go ahead and share what's on your mind?" Or "I think you had something you wanted to talk to me about." Obviously there is nothing magic about these phrases, and I know most of you can come up with your own. The main thing is to let the counselee know you are ready to listen.

If you asked the counselee to get together with you, you may need an additional sentence or two of introduction or explanation: "Bob, you were looking kind of down Sunday when we were visiting in the hallway at church. You mentioned that your work has become a real source of stress for you. I guess I was wondering if you would want to talk any more about that. I felt like we couldn't really get into anything in church."

Later we'll look at the difference between talking about yourself and talking about others, but for now, in order to get things started, you only need to demonstrate the willingness to listen and give the counselee permission to talk.

Keeping Things Going

It is not unusual for people to run out of things to say long before they have found out anything new about themselves or felt much better. When that happens, it is the counselor's job to keep them talking so they can express their feelings, and sometimes both counselor and counselee can figure out where the pain is coming from and possibly what to do about it.

A few little therapeutic tricks are virtually indispensable to the counselor in this "keep them talking" department. They are so simple, yet so powerful, you will find yourself using them in many conversations, even ones unrelated to counseling.

I am afraid that the simplicity of some of these things I will share and the obviously technical or functional focus may be offensive to some people. Some may feel it doesn't sound spiritual enough. Some of my recommendations may even sound like manipulation. I would like to remind you again of the attitude of depending on the Lord.

I want to help improve the counseling skill of God's people. There is no biblical basis for saying, "Trust God and don't worry about improving your skills." As I said earlier, no one would recommend that approach to a surgeon. It isn't recommended for people who cut through and try to remove emotional problem areas either. We are told to invest our talents and make them grow. Faith is vital, but faith without works is dead. So let's try to learn what we can to improve our skills, while not relying solely on skills and techniques. Our main source is always God.

First and best is simply to repeat the last word the other person says, often as a question. Here is an entire conversation with the counselor using this one technique.

WOMAN. Well, I had a terrible argument with Jim last night. We can't seem to settle on this thing with his driving.

COUNSELOR. Driving?

WOMAN. Yes, he won't drive the way I want him to, and he gets so defensive.

COUNSELOR. Defensive?

WOMAN. It's like nobody in the world is supposed to be able to be as good as he is. Mr. Wonderful!

COUNSELOR. Mr. Wonderful.

WOMAN. I get so tired of it. Usually I handle it all right, but in the car I really get afraid.

COUNSELOR. Afraid?

WOMAN. Yes, he drives way too fast.

I realize this example may seem a little stilted when you read it, but with natural tone inflections, it doesn't need to sound that way. In actual practice, you wouldn't use the same technique over and over. Sometimes you'd say, "Uh huh" or something like that, but the interesting thing is that people almost never have any idea what you are doing. Try it on your family tonight at dinner. If you can do it naturally, you will be amazed at how well it works to keep people talking. I once explained this technique to a pastoral counseling class, then called on a student and repeated his last word three sentences in a row. Each time he picked up again and talked more about what he had just said. I was surprised that even in that context, when I asked what technique I had been using just after describing it, neither he nor 50 percent of the class noticed. Here is another example:

MARGE. He was working from a wheelchair.
BILL. Wheelchair?
MARGE. Yes, when his leg was in a cast.
BILL. A cast?
MARGE. It was broken last year in a motorcycle accident.

Another idea to keep people talking is to repeat a key word or phrase. Here are some examples:

PATIENT. [*in hospital*] I don't know, I don't really have much on my heart today. Things look pretty good. I have been trying to get some of the other patients to go along to their groups. There is one woman who doesn't like them. She went to psychodrama the other day and she does like that, but she says she does not want to go to group therapy, so I was just trying to help her along with that.
DOCTOR. Trying to help.
PATIENT. It feels good if I accomplish something with them. I always try to do that. I have always tried to look out for everyone else, and that is where I have my problem. Sometimes I only care for other people and not myself.
DOCTOR. Others, not yourself.
PATIENT. Yeah, I get out of balance on that, I think. I have always been that way. If I want to do something and the person I am with wants to do something else, I always give in. After a while I am not even sure if I have opinions. It's like

I just do whatever my friend or family says is right.

DOCTOR. What *they* say is right.

PATIENT. That's how I got on drugs and skipped so much school that I finally dropped out. My friends said it was fun.

In a less clinical example let's look at two friends talking over coffee. We'll use both techniques we have introduced so far, the last word and the key word or phrase.

CAROL. I don't know what to do about dating Bob. He seems so persistent.

JOAN. Persistent?

CAROL. He calls me at least every other day. He doesn't pressure me or anything. He just asks how I am doing and acts like a friend.

JOAN. He doesn't pressure?

CAROL. No, I feel under pressure, but I don't think it's from him. It's from me.

JOAN. It's from you.

CAROL. Yeah, I hate to hear myself say this, but I know Bob is looking for a wife. He is a dentist, makes good money. He loves the Lord. He seems to be genuinely interested in me. He takes me to nice places. He never pressures me to do anything sexually. Frankly, he is ideal husband material, and my family and friends and my own common sense tell me I'm crazy if I don't grab him while I have the chance.

JOAN. You *hate* to hear yourself say it?

CAROL. It sounds so mercenary. I guess I just don't know how much of love is supposed to be based on such objective, commonsense stuff and how much should be based on my heart going flip-flop.

I have limited this example to two techniques we have used so far. In real life I probably wouldn't repeat the same technique several times in a row like that, but you can see that it works to keep the counselee talking.

Often the counselee is going to stop every few sentences, expecting something from you. This is where novice counselors frequently get confused and start giving advice, misunderstanding what the counselee wants. The counselee wants to tell the story and wants to know that you are listening and understanding what is being said. But the counselee should do most of the talking. As a counselor, therefore, you need to communicate that you are still paying attention, without intruding on the story or the emotional journey.

You can imagine how many well-meaning friends will succumb to the temptation to move right in after this example with Carol and the dentist and tell her what to do. But do we really want to take the responsibility of telling someone to go ahead and get married, even if there is no love? Do we really want to tell Carol to work on the relationship and see if the feelings come? Do we really want to tell her to walk away from it if her heart isn't doing flip-flops? Would Carol listen anyway? What if she did and was unhappy?

In a moment I will continue the example with Carol, but first I want to explain two more techniques. Most of the time counselees will let you know when it is your turn to say something. How? They stop talking. Your goal is to communicate that you hear and understand, as briefly as possible. Listening is not just done with the ears. It is done with the brain, the body, and even the mouth. You can communicate with a simple "Yes," "Uh huh," "Hmmm," "Oh?" and other brief sounds or words that show you are listening. I'll say more about the brain and the body later on in this chapter.

Another good technique is to restate the message or underlying implication that you hear. This is a good way to communicate that you understand and care. In addition to telling them what you think they are feeling, you can tell them what under-lying message, guideline, rule for living, or conflict you hear. Always keep in mind that you only have about one or two sentences at a time to do this.

Let's go back now to the example of Carol, her dentist, and Joan, and add the brief "I am listening" words and brief "this is what I am hearing" comments. We will pick up by repeating Carol's last comment.

CAROL. It sounds so mercenary. I guess I just don't know how much of love is supposed to be based on such objective, commonsense stuff and how much should be based on my heart going flip-flop.

JOAN. Yeah, tough question.

CAROL. I really respect Bob. And I feel like I can be myself around him. I like that. I don't get all nervous around him and not know how to act like I do when I am around some gorgeous guy. I know one of the reasons is that I don't think of Bob as gorgeous. He is nice looking and well groomed, but I have dated guys a lot better looking.

Notice, while I break in here for a moment, how important your next comment can be in influencing where Carol's conversation and even her thoughts go. I want to show you a few different counselor responses at this point in the conversation and demonstrate their impact. In each case I will start by repeating Carol's last line.

Response Example One

CAROL. I have dated guys a lot better looking.

JOAN. Better looking?

CAROL. Well, yes, you know in a Hollywood sort of way. Bob's looks are more homey I guess. Average. Well, no, I guess not average. I think he's nice looking. Better than average.

Response Example Two

CAROL. I have dated guys a lot better looking.
JOAN. A lot.
CAROL. Yeah. I don't know. Maybe I'm just trying to talk myself into something I really don't feel.

Response Example Three

CAROL. I have dated guys a lot better looking.
JOAN. Uh huh.
CAROL. I guess I'm not sure how important that is or should be to me.
JOAN. Should be?
CAROL. Should be. I think "should" has always been one of my problems. Should feel, should do, should think. It's like, no matter what decision I make, I can't please everybody's idea of what I should do.

Response Example Four

CAROL. I have dated guys a lot better looking.
JOAN. And I hear you saying that's important to you.
CAROL. It has been, yes. I think that's the problem. I am questioning my values. I have been growing spiritually this last year. Somehow, focusing on looks seems superficial.
JOAN. So looks shouldn't be important at all?
CAROL. Not as important as they have been, but it still is kind of important to me.
JOAN. So you really have two separate questions. One is

about your changing values and priorities, and another is about the way things are going with Bob.

I would like you to imagine yourself in a class or a seminar with me for a moment. I would pass out the text of these four examples and have a discussion about which ones you like or dislike and why. Keep a slip of paper or a bookmark in the pages with the examples and refer to them as we go on. Let's look at Response Example One.

In Example One Joan repeats Carol's last words and makes them a question. This causes Carol to reevaluate what she just said. It is a good thing to do because Carol finds herself defending Bob. The counselor might pursue that in future sentences with something like, "It sounds like you are defending Bob," and that might be helpful to Carol to examine why she was defending him.

In Example Two, by picking the key phrase "a lot" and repeating it, Joan has implied her own very strong-sounding opinion of Bob's looks. The effect is to strengthen the part of Carol that doubts Bob because of his appearance. You can see that the immediate effect is for Carol to back off from Bob. Isn't it interesting to see that literally one phrase from the friend/counselor with a critical implied message about Bob can have such an impact?

Example Three shows that a neutral comment (like "Uh huh") allows the counselee to pursue her own thoughts. She really summarizes her problem with the very next sentence after that neutral "Uh huh." She says, "I'm not sure how important that is or should be to me." This is a time of changing values for Carol. If the counselor can remember to guide and not drive, the counselor can have an impact on Carol's future life—not by telling Carol who to marry but by guiding her into the biblical basis for establishing the priorities in her life.

Carol probably has friends, perhaps at work, who will surely try to influence her to accept a worldly philosophy. What happens to Carol if there are no godly counselors to help her in such a vital area as establishing priorities? Also, Carol doesn't have to live by the counselor's priorities, so the counselor shouldn't preach. She needs someone to guide her through a process of establishing her own priorities.

When the counselor repeats "should be?" she is pointing out Carol's problems that have prevented her from developing her own priorities. Carol has tried to please everyone else. Future discussion with Carol might focus on this theme and the reality that Carol is responsible to please God first and her own common sense and better judgment second, and she is not responsible at all to please every relative or friend. Carol can never function as an adult until she realizes this.

In Example Four Joan is a little more active. She is following the understanding, reflective statement model I have stressed. By saying back to Carol what she is hearing, Joan helps Carol hear herself and really look at her own problems.

I particularly like the interpretation Joan gives at the end of Example Four. Joan hears correctly, I think, that the "who am I? what do I want out of life? what do I believe is important?" questions are all very important to Carol right now. Carol is trying to establish answers. Joan also hears that priority issues will have to be settled before any decision can be made about Bob.

What I hear from Carol is that the relationship with Bob is still quite new. Carol doesn't have any love feelings for Bob yet. But these feelings develop at different rates for different people. In every couple, one person fell in love before the other. That doesn't mean "give up." I would hope that Carol wouldn't make a premature decision either to commit herself to Bob or to break up with him. It is obvious she has some prioritizing to do first. I firmly believe that when an individual's priorities are clear, the decisions make themselves. Carol really needs to put her attention there right now and let the "Bob thing" run its natural course for the time being. Besides that, the worst thing a person can do for a new relationship is rush it or put pressure on it to produce a certain feeling. The chances are good that if Carol allows herself to date Bob for the fun and the friendship of it and promises herself to make no decision until her priorities are clear, she might well develop some affection out of the respect she already has for him.

How Long Should a Counseling Session Last?

Real counseling can take as short a time as a few minutes and as long a time as perhaps an hour and a half. Very rarely do I go as long as an hour and a half and then only in a crisis or a first session. When a novice counselor tells me he has had a troubled married couple in his living room, counseling with them for four hours, I usually shake my head in bewilderment. The only reasons I can see for that kind of marathon are (1) the counselor thought he could help resolve the whole marriage in one evening, (2) the counselor wasn't in control of the session and couldn't end it, or (3) he didn't know how to counsel.

Obviously I don't think anyone can help resolve serious marriage problems in one evening. On a rare occasion a counselor can fix an individual's problems in an evening if the individual is willing to make sudden, extreme, dramatic changes in life, such as moving out, kicking a roommate out, or quitting a job. Rarely, however, can both sides of a story be told in a single session. Rarely do both sides' strengths, weaknesses, attitudes, and willingness to change become evident in one evening. And rarely are problems so one-dimensional that a single environmental change makes it all better. Even if that counselor thought he knew what should be done in a single extended session, (1) he probably hasn't spent enough time with them to be sure, (2) he probably shouldn't tell other people what to do with their lives, and (3) after only one session, the counselee(s) won't trust him enough to do what he says anyway.

The general wisdom among professional counselors (which I subscribe to) is that an hour and a half may be appropriate for an initial session (I rarely take that long even then), but if something can't be said in an hour, it's too much for one session anyway. People only have a limited amount of emotional energy, and they can take only so much emotional nakedness at a time.

Informal counseling sessions where you meet someone at a restaurant for coffee and talk about the problem should still be limited to an hour. And don't be upset if it takes less time than that. If you feel you have come to a natural stopping place and the person has learned one thing new and has one new thing to work on, feel free to stop even if it has only been forty minutes or less.

In brief encounter counseling in the back of the church, you may only have two minutes. Beware of that and don't get into "why are you always down on yourself?" or "why do you hate your mother?" right there in church. You can still be understanding and caring in your listening and it is still helpful.

Ending a Counseling Session

Many novices let counseling sessions go on and on simply because they have no idea of how to end them. There are some simple ways to do this. If you remember the next few paragraphs, you will save yourself a lot of time and be more in control of your time and the counseling sessions.

I have arranged my office so that a clock sits in a bookcase just behind the counselee. That way I can glance over the counselee's shoulder and see the clock without being offensive. Trust me. If someone is talking and you look at your watch, you are giving a very clear body language message that says, "I want to get out of here!"

Once counselees have been seeing you for counseling for a few weeks, they will know to expect an hour. If they are offended because you give them only an hour of your time per week, that is their problem. It should be discussed openly in counseling. You might say that you have noticed they seem offended when counseling sessions end each week at an hour. Do they often have trouble accepting limits in relationships? Do they have a pattern of brief intense relationships that typically end badly?

Only in the first couple of counseling sessions, therefore, does the counselor have to worry about being really active in ending the session or about whether or not the counselee will be surprised by the session ending. If in the early sessions the counselor does give the counseling relationship the structure it needs (as in "we will meet each Tuesday from 7:00 to 8:00 P.M. at the restaurant to talk about this problem"), it will be far easier to control the counseling in later sessions.

In first sessions it is appropriate to warn or prepare the counselee that things are coming to a close for this week. I expect readers to come up with their own style and phrases, but here are some of the things that I do.

About five minutes before the end of the first session, I might say, "Well, Ron, I am starting to be concerned about our time here, let me ask you this...." or "Before we run out of time for today (we've got about five minutes left), tell me about...."

Another, more subtle way of terminating a session that I would use, both in earlier and in later sessions, is directing the counselee's conversation and thoughts toward the coming week or the session just being completed. Many people call it "summing up." Here is an example.

"I hear that there has been a theme tonight in much of what you have said. You have said that you tend to hold in all your negative thoughts, never expressing them and that you tend to get depressed right after that. This week, why don't you try to express your negative emotions in a controlled, positive way, like we talked about, and then next week when we get together again we can see how that went. Would you be willing to try to express yourself that way at least one time this week?"

You will find that a few people miss the "we're wrapping up now" message and they want to go on. They may say, "You know I've always had trouble with that. When I was a boy...." Feel free to interrupt at that point. This is what decides who is in control of the counseling. Interrupt and say, "Ron, excuse me, I want to make sure you have the time to finish that story. Shall we get together once next week so we can continue?"

As soon as you get your yes, the rest of your talk should be on structuring the next appointment.

Watch Out for the Rescuer

Don't, I repeat, don't tell counselees to drop by anytime! That is virtually always a mistake because you will get burned-out and end up not being a help to anyone. It is far kinder to everyone to suggest a specific time that is convenient to you. Remember, you are doing counselees a favor by listening to their problems and trying to help. You are probably doing this for free, so don't allow others to take unfair advantage of you. I am aware that I probably just offended some dear idealistic people, but once you have done this wrong and find out for yourself that feeling obligated to leave your son's birthday party to listen to somebody with the same problem for the third time in a week, you will realize that structuring the counseling to have a beginning and an ending is more loving than allowing yourself to be drained.

I have only thrown one person out of my counseling office in fifteen years. That was a woman I allowed to take advantage of me until I was victimized, and finally I exploded. She would show up for appointments an hour and a half late, expecting to be seen without paying anything toward the agreed-upon charge. (I do counseling as a profession, so I have to charge people.) Finally, after months of this, she started blaming me for some problems she had, and I blew up. I am not proud of that, but I have tried to learn from it.

Here is what I learned. There is an inevitable series of events that, once set into motion, always progresses toward the same conclusion. The series of events begins when you, the counselor, make yourself a rescuer. You become a rescuer when you accept the responsibility to fix someone else's problem. Healthy counseling accepts only the responsibility to try to help the counselee fix his own problem. There is a major difference between the two approaches.

Once you are the rescuer, you inevitably become the victim. You will be taken advantage of and misused. You see, when you communicate the message that you are going to be responsible for their rescue, counselees feel they don't have to be responsible anymore. It's *your* problem, so they let you do the work.

The last part of the inevitable series of consequences is that sooner or later you will do what I did when I threw that woman out of my office. I let out all of my frustration and anger on her at once. I became the persecutor. Yes, I ended up persecuting or hurting the very person I started out to rescue. Eventually you have to stop carrying people because they simply become too heavy. And when you stop carrying them, they get hurt.

I did not discover this pattern of human behavior. Someone showed it to me once, and I have found it to be true many times since then.

Questions in Counseling

Asking questions is an important part of counseling, but there are some helpful and some unhelpful ways of asking questions. It is certainly permissible to have an excellent hour counseling session without once asking a question. On the other hand, as we try to guide people into looking at themselves and try to fill in the gaps in our own understanding of what is happening, some questions are likely to come up.

Several times a week somebody will say to me, "I don't really know what to talk about today. Why don't you ask me questions?" People often want you to ask questions so they don't have to exert the energy to talk about painful things. The more questions you ask, the harder you work and the less the counselees work. When you ask a lot of questions, you probably feel as if you are the one trying to come up with an answer. Counseling is not supposed to be that way. You are supposed to help others answer their own questions. You may clarify what answers they are seeking, but you are not supposed to be the answer person or the question person. As the counselor, you are to be the facilitator and make it easier for the counselees to ask and answer their own life questions.

Here is an example of an extended conversation with a counselee. You will see that when questions are asked, they are always intended to guide. A good question is usually a way of giving new information to a counselee or of gaining a new perspective. You will also notice that the problem here is depression. Depressed people tend to be low in energy. They may often wind down in counseling from time to time and may require some questions to keep them going or get them going again.

DR. FOSTER. So how are you?

KAY. I feel better today. I have been reading your book on depression and thinking about that and also what we talked about last time. Of course, I deal with my ups and downs like I said and I've been feeling fine so far. Half an hour from now I could go to my room and cry. My moods just change so quick. It seems as long as I have someone to keep me busy....I have been reading that book since after breakfast, therefore I haven't had anything on my mind, nothing to be depressed about. I don't know. I don't know what else to talk about.

DR. FOSTER. You said you were thinking a lot about what we talked about yesterday. What about that?

KAY. Well, I have to start thinking more of myself and putting myself more ahead of other people. Last night I thought a lot about that. Most of the time I just don't say anything about what I want. I just don't get anywhere.

DR. FOSTER. You say you don't get anywhere. What does that mean?

KAY. Well, usually some things that I talked about with Tony about my life when I was small, he'd just say, "Well, you're pitying yourself. Just don't think about it." And I tried not to think about it, but it's always been there. And different things, as far as feelings. Sometimes I felt like I had to get out of the house and be alone, just for awhile. He felt that wasn't right because I am a mother and I should be with my children all the time and not feel like I need time alone. It is just things like that, and then after awhile I don't ask for anything and don't say what I am feeling.

DR. FOSTER. You just kind of give up?

KAY. Yeah.

DR. FOSTER. I wonder if there is any connection between giving up on trying to meet your own needs and then later getting depressed?

KAY. Yeah. I know I used to feel depressed a lot because I had felt different needs that I had and felt that I couldn't do them and sometimes I got depressed about those things. As far as accomplishments, I feel like I have never accomplished anything and that depresses me a lot. We talked about that yesterday, when I start something, I seem to never get finished with it somehow. I always have big plans to do something, but I never follow through with them. I

51

don't know what else to talk about.

DR. FOSTER. The reason I asked you before about what you meant when you said you didn't get anywhere is because most people think that the reason they are supposed to say what they feel is so that *other* people will change. Sometimes other people change, sometimes they don't. But if your health depends on what they do, you end up being victimized. Your health really can depend on what *you* do, whether you express yourself or whether you don't, with or without their approval. That's been kind of hard for you to do so far.

KAY. Yeah.

DR. FOSTER. In other words, your own common sense told you that as a mother, twenty-four hours a day, seven days a week is too much time with the kids. It will make you crazy. You knew that, your own common sense knew that. But you took somebody else's opinion rather than your own.

KAY. Yeah. Well, not only Tony but a lot of other people said this. Most of my family believes that this is the place for a mother, at home and only at home. If I go somewhere, my children should be with me. By the end of some days, I felt like I was going to bang my head into the wall. I just couldn't take it anymore. Then I felt guilty. After I was done yelling at the kids all day, I didn't feel like sitting and talking with them, trying to explain, because I wasn't getting anywhere and I was getting frustrated with myself because I felt like I was not accomplishing anything with them. So then, eventually, it ended up that I was just yelling and yelling. Then when they were ready to go to bed at night, I was relieved and yet I felt guilty at the same time. I don't know. Sometimes I don't know if I have those feelings, if they are right, that I need time away, because everybody else is telling me that it's not right.

DR. FOSTER. I am not your judge and I can't tell you what to do, but I know that other people can't look inside you and see what your needs are either.

KAY. I see other people so happy just being with their children and they always want to be with them, and they don't need time away.

DR. FOSTER. And because they can do it twenty-four hours a day, therefore you should be able to?

KAY. I guess.

DR. FOSTER. Are you like everybody else?

KAY. I feel that I have too much influence from other people. I feel like everyone else is telling me what they think is right so I try to listen to what they say. But I want to be a good person, and I don't know if these feelings I have are good.

DR. FOSTER. Repeated questions come up, "Am I okay? Are my feelings right or wrong? Should I do what I think I should do or what others tell me?" These are themes that come through pretty often.

KAY. I guess I have to somehow make that decision. I can't stop my feelings or how I feel inside. Like I was saying when I was taking drugs and things before I knew it was wrong but I kept doing it. Eventually I got myself out of it, and I knew that was the right thing to do. But now, from everyone telling me what to do and "this is the right thing, or you should do...," they have just convinced me so often that I now cannot make my own decisions.

DR. FOSTER. It's almost as if you have taken the power of choice over yourself and given it away to other people. This sounds like a constant struggle.

KAY. Yeah.

DR. FOSTER. That makes you unhappy with yourself. You feel like a victim. Why would anybody do that? Why would someone take power of choice and give it away?

KAY. You know, I always felt like I wanted to please other people. I guess because I want to make people happy mainly because I was unhappy, yet I try to make them happy. That does not make sense to me because no matter how hard I try, I am not happy with myself. Right now, I am just trying to work on myself and how to feel better about myself. I think that is the most important thing right now. Then maybe later I can deal with some other things. It is confusing too, for me, sometimes because I don't know what to work on first. So I just forget about the past and just look to the future. Am I going to be able to forget about that? When I feel I'm okay, am I going to go home and not take anything personally? I've got to have enough confidence in myself that I won't do that.

DR. FOSTER. I guess the answer to that is that it is up to you whether you go home and go back to the old you or try some new things.

KAY. I have to learn to be strong. I haven't been.

DR. FOSTER. You felt like you must please everyone else, you must make other people like you, you must do what they think.

KAY. Either that or I'll lose my friends.

DR. FOSTER. Yes, very much so. And it's gotten you on drugs so far, and on other things that you really wish you had not been involved in. I guess I would like you to evaluate your rules for living and maybe see if there are some rules that don't particularly make sense. It sounds to me as if you are questioning those rules. Particularly the "I must please everyone" rule and the "my feelings and opinions don't really count" rule.

A look at this session shows that my questions included, "What does that mean?" "Are you like everybody else?" and "Why would anybody do that?" One of these is a closed question. A closed question requires a yes or no answer rather than asks for further explanation. Once in a while a closed question can be effective, such as in this case, "Are you like everybody else?" Frequently a closed question is effective when it is meant to be more of a statement (as it was in this case) than a question. The counselee was to say, "No, I am different from other people." I was trying to get her to see a particular idea. Most of the time, however, open questions are far more effective in getting counselees to look at themselves and their feelings and behaviors.

The next example is of bad questioning techniques. You will notice it includes another kind of closed question—the multiple choice. You can see how hard the counselor is working and how little the counselee is examining herself.

COUNSELOR. Tell me. Did you feel better after leaving your mother?

COUNSELEE. No.

COUNSELOR. Did you feel like she took advantage of you again?

COUNSELEE. Yes.

COUNSELOR. Did you want to go back and yell at her, give up, or get depressed, or what?

COUNSELEE. I don't know.

COUNSELOR. Sometimes do you just want to tell your mother off?

COUNSELEE. I guess so. I don't know.

This is ineffective counseling. Make sure the counselees do most of the talking. They are supposed to be evaluating their lives.

Don't be Afraid of Silences

When a counselor gets anxious during a time of silence in a session, the counselor is likely to try to fill in the silence with talking or trying to get the counselee to talk. This may include a lot of poor questions, as we have just seen. The counselor must always remember who owns the problem. If something is the counselee's problem, then the counselee should work on it. If it is not the counselee's problem, the counselee needs to let go of it. The counselor helps no one by making the counselee's problem his own.

If the counselee is stuck, it is appropriate for the counselor to try to get the session moving. But "helping" is different from "driving." I suggest comments like, "I wonder what you are feeling right now?" or "It might be good if you would do some of that thinking out loud." But that's about it. If it's hard for someone to talk, but the person is trying, wait. If counselees don't want to be in counseling, that's their business. They don't have to tell you everything.

One other thought on silences. Sometimes a counselee who was previously talking suddenly becomes quiet because a counselor said something that caused anger. You might suggest that that may be what happened and ask about it. If you can remember the last thing you said or the last thing the counselee said, that might give you enough of a clue to guess what the counselee is feeling.

Do Listen for What Isn't There

My family and I lived in a lovely brick home in Hershey that has a lot of history. The original owner of the house tells in the foreword of a book he wrote on the life of Milton S. Hershey (the candy bar man) that he was almost finished with the book when there was a great explosion in which the printing press, all the text already completed, and both of the author/printer's legs were destroyed. The interesting thing is that the author fails to mention that his wife was killed in the explosion. You can infer a lot from what isn't said.

If the counselee has been talking for an hour about his background, his family, and so on and never mentions his father, I have to assume dad was emotionally absent. Of course, this would be true for any other significant individual who is being left out of the discussion. Sometimes it can be very interesting detective work to listen for what is not being said.

Do Watch Carefully

We counselors need to watch our own bodies and what they are saying as well as those of our counselees. If a problem suddenly develops in counseling, you can usually see a sign of it in the counselee's body. I am not going to try to do a whole book on body language in a few paragraphs, but I want to emphasize that you should really watch your counselees. Notice whether they are facing you or turned halfway away. If you are working with a couple, notice how they sit in relationship to each other. Watch their arms. Do they reach out? Watch their legs. Are they crossed? Look for changes. They will often indicate anxiety, defensiveness, anger, caution, or other emotions. You need to note not only what their bodies do, but also at what point in the conversation it occurs. What you see is not so much a fact as an indication or a signpost. It gives you reason to ask questions.

Your own body is also important to watch. Are you feeling tired or bored? Is your mind wandering? These are indications of what is happening (or not happening) in the counseling. If you feel bored, the chances are good that the counselee is not saying anything new but rather repeating something that has been said many times. It is your job, then, to try to get the counselee out of the rehearsed lines into some real thinking.

When ending a session, you can communicate that by sitting forward in your chair, by picking up a pencil and an appointment book, and even by getting up from your chair as you start talking about the time for the next session.

I handle one of the ticklish situations in counseling totally with body language. Once in a while a counselee stands up when I do, but then continues to talk, hoping for an extra twenty minutes of counsel while we both stand. I just open the door and start walking down the hall. Of course, the counselee follows. Then I stop, back into my room, and gently close the door, nodding pleasantly all the way, saying while I close the door, "Yes we will have to talk about that next time." That may sound abrupt or even offensive to some people, but you must understand that if I am unable to end an appointment at a scheduled time, I am then automatically being rude to the person scheduled as my next appointment. If I was twenty minutes late for my first appointment in the morning, that could make me twenty minutes late for everyone during the day. Or, if I ran twenty minutes long for each appointment I could be up to two hours late by the end of the day. In the long run, for most people, it is more loving for the counselor simply to be in control of the session and to start and stop as promptly as possible.

In summary, techniques to keep the counselee talking include repeating the last word, key word, or phrase, and communicating that you are listening, sometimes by restating what you are hearing. In structuring the interview, the counselor should be aware of the dangers of rescuing and the importance of guiding.

5

How Emotions Work

If we were studying how to repair televisions rather than how to counsel (repair emotions), I think much of our study would focus upon working televisions rather than broken ones. I remember, as a boy, taking apart a broken carburetor. I could take it apart just fine, but I couldn't fix it. Know why? I didn't know how it worked when it wasn't broken. In this chapter I will explain how healthy emotions work and then describe how they become unhealthy.

Emotional Reflexes

An *emotion* is "an internal movement or reaction." God has designed us so that we have many automatic reactions. Some are learned. You know that if the doctor hits your knee in a certain spot with a little hammer, your lower leg is going to kick out. That is a reflex. If you voluntarily hold your breath long enough, you will faint (lose conscious control over your muscles) so that your body can continue breathing. This is an automatic reflex to protect the body.

You may have heard of the little boy who was drowned in icy water. When his body could no longer breathe, his mind shut off all but a few basic bodily functions and slowed them down dramatically, so that when he was resuscitated after twenty minutes under the water, he survived and was able to regain full bodily functions. As you can see, reflexes are automatic and built in for the preservation of the organism. Emotions are reflexes. If we learn how they work, we can really learn to help people.

That emotions are automatic is important to remember, especially for Christians. Some Christians tend to be judgmental, mentally putting tags of right and wrong on areas of life including emotions. But I question the rightness or wrongness of automatic reflexes. Oh yes, I know that some of the things we do with our emotions can be right or wrong, and some of the attitudes that precede our emotions are also right or wrong, but I am not so sure that that is true about the emotions themselves.

This is important to establish because so many people say, "I am not supposed to be angry. So I won't talk about it because anger is a sin." Hiding emotions, even if the emotion can be called sinful, often leads to emotionally unhealthy behaviors. We as Christians are told to confess our sins, not hide them. So even if an emotion would be sinful, hiding it would be an inappropriate response. I am convinced that there is no basic conflict between a proper understanding of emotional health and living biblically. Let's look at healthy emotions.

Normal emotional functioning produces an emotion every several minutes. There may be times and situations when you seem to be producing several conflicting emotions at the same time, and you may have very quiet times when you may produce only a few emotions per hour. But let's say for the sake of argument that one emotion is manufactured every ten minutes.

In normal emotional functioning (by "normal," I mean "healthy"), that emotion is sent from the production line to the packaging and labeling department where it is given a name ("Uh huh, I am feeling hurt...") and an address ("...at Jane for not speaking to me"). From the packaging and labeling department, the emotion goes to the shipping and delivery department where it can be expressed ("Jane, I was hurt yesterday when I felt you wouldn't talk to me").

Like most analogies, this one eventually breaks down because not every emotion is intended to be expressed. We don't always have others around so that we can say what we feel, and six emotional statements per hour would not be normal either. But if an emotion is significant, we must express it or deliver it in some way. How can we tell if an emotion is significant? If it is very intense, it should usually be expressed. If it still bothers us several hours or perhaps a day later, it should usually be expressed.

Just a few minutes after an emotion is properly expressed, that emotion starts to dissipate. Almost as soon as an emotion comes out of our mouths, it starts to fade. This is healthy emotional functioning: admitting, talking about, noticing, expressing, and confessing what we feel.

Emotional Logjams

Go back to the analogy of a factory where a new emotion is produced every ten minutes. What would happen if the shipping and delivery department went on strike, but the emotions plant continued to produce emotions? Soon the storeroom would be full, and you would have to start piling boxes inside the factory. The boxes would start to clog the assembly line, and eventually the whole system would shut down.

What I have just described is the general cause of most depression. As the system gets clogged, a person can no longer feel emotions. A depressed person is apathetic. "I just don't care about things anymore. It's like a part of me is dead." A feeling of the "blahs" is phase one of depression.

Other symptoms include a change in appetite (not eating or eating constantly); a change in sleeping patterns (difficulty sleeping or sleeping too much); and a change in crying patterns (crying all the time, feeling the need to cry but being unable to do so, or not crying at all when it's normal for an individual to cry).

A feeling of being overly self-conscious is another symptom of depression. You may be doing exactly what you normally do, but you may feel as though people are watching you or as though you no longer fit in. Many things you do each day are done more or less on automatic pilot. When you are depressed, it is as if your automatic pilot is broken and you have to do everything on "manual." Another symptom is the loss of confidence, and finally, a drop in mood produces sad feelings.

Sometimes a really big emotion is produced, such as grief over a loss. When that emotion can't make it through the emotional pipeline, it can clog up the whole emotional system. When this occurs, the person may need a counselor (emotional plumber) to pull out first one emotion and then another. This continues until the depressed person is able to bring out, express, and feel what couldn't be handled the first time. Until that emotion is felt and dealt with, the depressed person is going to continue to be stuck. I might add that the sooner the emotion or situation is identified, the easier it is to get unstuck.

If a friend says that he has been feeling down the last couple of days, try to help him pinpoint the first time he noticed feeling down or the last time he remembers feeling good, then backtrack to what events happened since the last time he felt good. You will usually be able to find an event that produced an emotion. Not only that, but you will find it was an emotion that he didn't really handle well. He probably just walked away, saying nothing to the other person but saying to himself, *Don't make trouble. Just forget about it.*

People give that advice quite often, to themselves and to others, and it is rarely good advice. By holding in something and not dealing with it, we make quite a bit of emotional trouble for ourselves.

Attitudes Precede Emotions

I suggested that emotions are automatic. I believe that. Once you feel something, you don't get rid of it by ignoring it. Just hoping that something will go away is not a good problem-solving technique. Once you are angry, you have to acknowledge that anger (confess it, if you will) or do something with it. However, if you notice that you tend to get angry often, you might ask yourself why. The answer to that lies with the *attitude* that preceded your emotion. An *attitude* is the way you view yourself, God, others, and the world.

When you walk into a room, you walk into a situation or a circumstance. How you react to that situation produces a reflex called an emotion. Then you produce an emotional expression. Someone might say, "Well, then, you see! I really can't control what I feel or how I react, so why blame me?"

There are places in the process that you can control what your emotional output is likely to be. Look at this diagram.

Attitude
↓
Environment or Situation
↓
Internal Emotional Response
↓
Emotional Expression

When you walk into an environment or a situation, you bring with you an attitude. What is an attitude? It is the way you view yourself, God, others, and the world around you. Attitudes are changeable. Let's look at two examples.

In the first example, Alecia walks into a restaurant lobby

where several people are sitting. One of them asks her if she is eating alone and asks if she would like to join him. Alecia smiles pleasantly, says, "Thank you, but I am waiting for a friend," and enjoys her lunch. She tells her girlfriend, "I guess I don't look too bad. A man asked me to lunch while I was waiting for you." Alecia's only emotion in the situation was to feel complimented.

In the second example, Margo walks into the same restaurant lobby and is asked by the same man if she is eating alone and if she would like to join him. Margo reacts instantly, raises her eyebrows, and says icily, "No, I would not!" Margo's lunch is ruined. She spends the whole time fuming to her girlfriend, "Why can't a girl go out and have a nice quiet lunch without being hit on! It's a disgrace. In broad daylight! And the man must have been twenty years older than me. He is probably on a pass from the home for dirty old men."

Obviously the two women walked into the room with very different attitudes, yet both emotional reflexes were automatic. Alecia has a very warm, loving family, a great relationship with her dad and two brothers. Margo's dad left her mother and her and her two sisters for another woman. Margo is "preset" to be angry because of how she looks at the world in general and men in particular.

Did anyone ever preach at you when you were feeling depressed, disappointed, or angry? Did you ever wonder why the preaching seemed to do no good when you were already angry? That was because your problem was between the emotional reflex and the emotional expression, and the preaching was aimed at the attitude that preceded the whole process. It is very hard to fix an emotional expression problem by changing an attitude. That is like filling in the cavity in a tooth the dentist just pulled. It's too late for attitude adjustment when what you need is expression adjustment. A person who is upset may need some attitude altering to prevent that from happening again, but at the moment some emotional expression lessons are required, not sermons about attitude.

This process is greatly misunderstood, and a lot of well-meaning, would-be counselors preach about attitudes when what people really need at the moment is to let out some steam and reduce their internal pressure.

The Emotional Pressure Cooker

Do you know what a pressure cooker looks like? I bought one a few years ago at a flea market, and I use it to show people what they are doing to themselves when they hold everything inside. Here is a drawing of a pressure cooker.

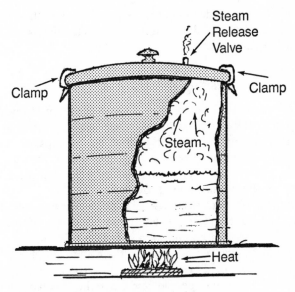

Pressure Cooker

I often pull out the pressure cooker, and while tapping the steam release valve I'll ask, "What would happen if you put this pot on the stove and clamped down the lid, but the steam release valve was stuck shut?"

The counselees usually say, "There would be an explosion." That is right, there will be, or in some situations perhaps an implosion where the sides just cave in.

"When you don't tell your boss (mother, spouse, or whoever) exactly what you feel and you get really steamed up over something, the same thing happens to you. Your pressure builds up and you may explode." I then tell my counselees, "What we have to do to fix this problem and prevent new emotional problems is to install a pressure release valve in you. You either don't have one or yours is stuck."

People seem to understand this explanation, and they have a clearer idea of the goal in counseling. What follows is God's pressure release valve.

Speaking the Truth in Love

In Ephesians 4:15 we are told to speak the truth in love. No particular fanfare is given to this verse, and the truth is certainly taught in other parts of the Bible, but perhaps nowhere is the key to godly emotional expression and communication given in a more clear, concise form. Our communication is to be twofold, both truthful and loving.

Look what happens when we try to apply just one-half of the verse. No matter which half we try to apply, truthfulness or love, it gets unbalanced and topples without the other.

Carl and Nancy met a couple in their adult Sunday school class they think might become really good friends. George and Chris seemed to be nice people, and when they invited Carl and Nancy over for the evening, they all had a great time. Before leaving, Carl and Nancy invited them to dinner the following Saturday.

Nancy worked hard at making a nice dinner, but George and Chris were forty-five minutes late. They apologized and it was forgotten, but three weeks later when George and Chris were to come again, they were more than a half-hour late.

Nancy and Carl were very prompt people, and Nancy typically planned a meal to be ready five to ten minutes after the guests' appointed arrival time. She was quite annoyed at the lateness, and the evening didn't go as well as the previous evening had. After George and Chris left, Carl and Nancy talked. What should they do? Their options and the inevitable results of each are quite clear.

They could deny that they are upset and say nothing, hoping to preserve their friendship and not risk hurting feelings. But the inevitable consequence of this is a lack of openness in the relationship. George and Chris won't know why, but relationships will be a little bit colder. What's worse, every unexpressed negative emotion will become another brick in the wall between the two couples. Eventually the wall will get so high that no love can get through it anymore, and the relationship will die. The tragic thing is that the couple was well motivated when they decided not to be truthful. They didn't want to offend or cause trouble.

Another option might have been for Carl and Nancy to have it out with George and Chris right then and there, when they were angry. What would have happened if Carl and Nancy expressed the anger truthfully, but without love? It would have been destructive. There might have been name calling and accusations. There would most definitely be hurt feelings and obviously a hurt relationship. No, blowing up is not the answer.

The biblical guideline of speaking the truth in love is easy to teach and easy to remember, and it works so well that it is a real tribute to the One whose truth it is. Here is an example of Carl and Nancy speaking the truth in love to George and Chris.

"We came over tonight because we need to talk to you both. The other night we were feeling annoyed by your being over a half-hour late to dinner. I think that was made worse by the fact that you were late the first time you came over to dinner too, and we didn't say anything about it. We talked about what to do and realized that we don't want to lose you as friends. We really feel close to you. We have been looking for a couple that we felt comfortable with. So, even though it's kind of embarrassing and threatening to come over and say, 'Hey, we're angry. We don't like lateness,' we thought that we had to deal with our anger as soon as we could, to get rid of it. We felt really lonely since the other night, and we just decided that being close to you was worth the risk, so we thought we would come over and tell you how we felt."

I hardly need to add my two cents to that. God's truth speaks for itself. We need to practice doing this with every relationship worth saving. Then, as counselors, we need to use this verse as a guideline in our communication with our counselees, and we need to diligently teach it as the preferred method of communication and the preferred pressure release valve for our counselees.

Many Symptoms from One Cause

You will be continually surprised at how many different problems and symptoms can be and will be cured if the people you counsel will learn to handle their emotions in this way. By doing so, they can become unstuck, internal pressure is released, symptoms decrease and/or disappear, and their lives are genuinely changed. The following cases are similar to ones I have dealt with that became cured after the people got the courage, the ability, and the will to speak the truth in love.

• A twenty-eight-year-old accountant was having sudden periods of weakness and dizziness. The attacks were so bad that he would have to grab a chair or lean against the wall to keep from falling over. He discovered that he had these spells immediately after he had gotten annoyed at something but had not expressed that annoyance.

• A twenty-four-year-old housewife was afraid to drive because she had an intense impulse to run the car into people. Although she never did anything dangerous or harmful to other people, she lived in constant fear that she might.

• A forty-year-old mother had sudden, acute anxiety attacks. She would go into extreme panic, hyperventilate, and believe that she was dying.

• A thirty-five-year-old merchant became so depressed he couldn't go to work anymore. He had crying spells and felt a complete loss of self-confidence.

• A thirty-three-year-old father had problems with his temper. He typically held everything in for several days or several weeks, but when he lost control, his anger exploded in incredibly destructive outbursts. Before counseling, he had always reacted by feeling guilty and promised himself each time that he would not let his anger out again. He had to learn that by clamping the lid down too tightly, he was guaranteeing that sooner or later the pressure would build up and he would explode again.

Please don't misunderstand. There is more to counseling than saying this one little truth and expecting miracles. You guide gently; you reinforce attempts at change. You suggest alternative methods, and you pray and wait. Also, obviously there are other emotional problems than the ones caused by this one truth. But understanding the pressure cooker theory is central to successful counseling.

Running Out of Troops

Another major result of holding in emotions and getting an emotional logjam is what I call "running out of troops." Here is what I mean. Take your hands and press them together. Push them really hard. You will notice that while you are exerting a lot of energy, you are not really accomplishing any work. When a particular emotion is trying to come out and you exert equal force to keep that emotion in, you are doing the same thing to yourself.

Let's imagine for a moment that we are all given 100 troops' worth of emotional and physical energy to fight our daily battles. That should be more than enough to get through any crisis *if* we handle our crises one at a time.

Suppose you have a medium-sized problem, such as being fired, which you refuse to deal with emotionally. You just won't acknowledge your feelings. If this is a 15-troop problem and you don't finish the battle, you have to leave 15 troops behind to keep that problem below your level of consciousness. That is 15 plus 15, so you have depleted your troops by 30 and have only 70 left to fight your daily battles.

That is still enough troops to handle most anything. But then your mother dies—a 25-troop problem—and you don't let yourself feel that feeling either. You think that you are too busy making arrangements to fall apart now, so you have to leave 25 troops behind to push down that 25-troop problem. This costs you 50 more troops, and you are now down to 20.

It takes about 10 troops just to get up in the morning, look yourself in the mirror, and face the world. If you spend 2 here and 3 there, not feeling things, pretty soon you are running on empty. For a little while you can borrow on tomorrow's troops, but sooner or later you have nothing left to borrow. You wake up one morning, needing 10 troops to face the day, and you've only got 6. You roll over, pull the blanket over your head, and say, "I just can't cope."

A loss of energy is a significant emotional symptom. It often means that the person is out of troops. Therapy for these individuals involves going back and feeling those things that were not felt the first time. This may include saying good-by to a deceased mother, facing the loss and hurt that someone loved doesn't return that love, or confronting many other painful emotions. But even though facing these painful things hurts terribly, it is a temporary hurt that can be overcome. The hurt from the depression just goes on and on until someone steps in and helps unclog the emotional logjam.

As counselors, we are sometimes comforters of those in pain, but other times we are more like surgeons, even purposely causing pain (that is, helping people face their pain) in order to remove something that is damaging. Knowing when to do what is partly a matter of experience, partly a matter of dependence on God's leading, and partly a matter of understanding how healthy emotions work. As we understand healthy emotions we can try to guide the counselees toward functioning the way they were designed.

6

The Limitations of Counseling

When I tell my friends who are psychologists and psychiatrists about this book, they obviously don't all react the same way. However, most of them express concern that novice counselors might get in over their heads and end up doing damage to themselves or their counselees, especially counselees who are inclined to be self-destructive. I am concerned about that too. Probably very few people reading this book have ever had someone they were counseling commit suicide. Although I have never had that happen while I was currently working with someone, it has happened to two people I had worked with a year or two prior to their suicides. The odds are heavily against your having to deal with such situations, but I think it is best to be prepared for as many possibilities as you can be. In addition to suicide prevention, other issues I will discuss in this chapter include how to avoid getting counselor burn-out and how to go about referring a counselee who needs further help.

When to Refer: General Comments

Two marks of a well-trained person in almost any field are recognizing personal limitations and knowing when to refer to someone else. The field of mental health is no exception.

I don't mean that people without doctorates shouldn't be counseling. I have already made it clear that all of us as Christians should have some counseling skills so that we may adequately represent our Wonderful Counselor to the world. But we must all learn to recognize and live within our limitations. What happens to a pastor, a mother, or anyone who never says no? They get in trouble.

Why wouldn't a counselor admit that a particular problem was beyond his abilities? I can think of only a few reasons: (1) the counselor didn't know he couldn't handle it; (2) the counselor didn't want to admit he had limits; or (3) the counselor didn't want to hurt someone by saying no.

First, I am going to try to cover many of the areas that the typical Christian worker cannot handle so that those who have read this book will know when to ask for help. Second, only God is infinite, only He is without limits; we can't minister very well when our pride distorts our view of ourselves. Third, we need to realize that we hurt people far more by not being truthful with them than we do by saying no. As we saw in Chapter 5, speaking the truth in love is the biblical guideline. If we really want to help people, sometimes we have to help them hurt. This statement may be hard for some readers to accept, but remember, a hurt that is faced is a temporary hurt. That hurt starts to heal as soon as it is faced. A denied hurt, a refusal to face an emotion, can lead to problems that can go on and on. In other words, it is often far more loving to tell someone that we cannot give counsel than it is to try to do something that is not reasonably within our abilities.

In general, we need to refer counselees that we know we can't help. Oh yes, on some level, we know that God does the healing, and we are inadequate for anything by ourselves. But I am talking about a different level here. I am talking about each of us looking inside and asking, *Do I know what I am doing? Do I have a plan? Do I feel in control?*

If you feel out of control, you probably are out of control and should consider referring the counselee to someone with more training. Notice how you feel before, during, and after a counseling session. Are you unduly afraid? Do you ever feel desperate? Have you tried several different approaches, but you are out of ideas and nothing seems to work? Is the counselee showing signs of improvement at all after several sessions? Any of these conditions could mean that you should refer this counselee to someone with more training.

When to Refer: A Specific List

It would be impossible for me to compile a comprehensive list of when to refer counselees because there are so many variables. If I have omitted a problem category you are working with, I hope you will evaluate the situation carefully. If you are uncertain, you would probably be well advised to seek a professional's help.

You should refer people whose emotional-mental problems are causing them to break laws. This includes but is not limited to child molesters, compulsive gamblers, spouse abusers, and kleptomaniacs (people who compulsively steal). Also refer immediately anyone who tells you of plans to harm someone or to break the law.

Refer anyone you are afraid of or anyone you often find yourself angry with. The category of people you are afraid of doesn't include just people who threaten you. They may be people you are attracted to and afraid you might get emotionally and/or romantically involved with. I have said elsewhere in this book, and I say again, that lay counselors should work only with people of their own sex and pastoral counselors should take significant precautions when working with people of the opposite sex.

If you are in a ministry or a profession in which counseling people of the opposite sex is expected as part of your job, you must be very careful to protect yourself in every way possible.

If you notice you dress with a particular counselee in mind or you think or fantasize about that person, refer the counselee to someone else. You might hurt the counselee, who might not understand what is happening, but that is still a little hurt in order to prevent a big hurt. It is better for both of you if you make a referral.

Someone is going to ask, "Why shouldn't I just tell the other person the real reason that I am making a referral? What about speaking the truth in love?" If you are attracted to a counselee, a part of your heart wants to confess its love. Once you have stated the real reason for the referral to the other person, in some way the attraction is more real and its expression has to affect your relationship. Once your reason has been stated, it must be dealt with. You would be far better off not to get into the situation in the first place. Besides the pain involved, once you experience romantic feelings about someone, you have lost your objectivity as a counselor. Your helpfulness will be highly questionable.

The Suicidal Person

Refer to a trained professional therapist, a psychologist, or a psychiatrist anyone who is suicidal. How do you know if someone is suicidal? Ask a straightforward question about the subject. Most people have had a suicidal thought fly through their heads for a brief second. If that thought doesn't really land, it just flew through, then the person doesn't really qualify as suicidal. If someone admits to sitting down and thinking about suicide for a period of time, contemplating its advantages and disadvantages, that person is close enough to being suicidal to merit a referral.

Ask counselees if they have thought about how they would take their own lives. In general, someone who has not thought about a specific plan is not nearly as serious a risk as someone who has developed one. If the counselee has a plan, refer.

Of course, not everyone contemplating suicide will admit it to you. Then what do you do? You look for other signs. Sometimes when someone who has been depressed for a long time finally makes the decision to end it all, an immediate lift in mood becomes apparent. It comes from the thought, *Well, I have a plan. I have decided, and I won't have to put up with this world much longer.* If you are counseling with someone who suddenly changes behavior, you might become suspicious and ask questions about suicide.

Also, it is certainly not true that those who talk about suicide don't do it. A vast majority of people who have actually attempted suicide have given a warning of some kind. It is not unusual for a suicidal person to get financial affairs all organized or to suddenly pay off all debts. People often wait months or even years for a big bonus, a settled lawsuit, or some other big financial payoff. They think that by paying off (they call it "giving to") their relatives, the relatives won't be mad at them. If you pursue their reasoning, you will often find that they think their family members will finally love them.

Suicide is often a very angry act. Like many depressed people, those who take their own lives are angry. Rather than let the anger out, they clamp the lid down and turn that anger in on themselves. When that hits the lid, it has nowhere else to go but to turn back on them. Suicide is often a statement that says, "I am so angry at you I could kill (me)." These people turn the anger in on themselves because that is what they have always done with their anger.

In other cases, suicidal persons are trying not to seek love but to strike a blow. They are trying to make others feel guilty and miserable. *When I'm gone, they will be sorry for the way they treated me,* they say to themselves. Still, underneath that feeling is often the unconscious hope that the family will then, after being sorry, embrace them in arms of love to make everything all right. Many suicidal people don't really realize that they won't be around for that last act. They will be dead, and the family's imagined renewed love won't do them any good.

It is true that many families do feel guilty after a suicide, but if the suicidal person was never truly loved or accepted by the family before the suicide, he is unlikely to be loved any more afterward. A more typical reaction from unloving families is, "She never was normal. Always a little different, a little strange, a little crazy. The suicide just proves it." Yes, the fact is that suicides rarely, if ever, improve a family's feelings about an individual. If a family loved before, they forgive and love after. If they didn't love before, they still won't. This is a good point for a counselor to talk through with a person who has suicidal feelings. Nevertheless, it is still my opinion that nonprofessionals should not work with suicidal people. The risk is simply too great, and the pain isn't worth it. You may be called upon to do one-time crisis counseling with a suicidal person, however.

The Self-Abusing Person

The lay counselor should also avoid the self-abusing person. These people intentionally harm themselves. Why do they do it? They feel better afterward. In some cases, they feel so guilty about simple, minor, normal things that they relieve the guilt with pain (punishment). In other cases, they say that they feel nothing and that self-inflicted pain is the only way they can feel anything. If you find any counselees doing this, make a referral. These individuals are basically too sick for you as a nonprofessional to work with.

Self-abusing people are probably the most difficult to counsel, no matter what one's level of training. They constantly give double messages. For instance, a self-abusing counselee might make an appointment and then cancel. This person might come to talk to you but then stand on the other side of the room rather than sit. This person might talk very little and then later in the week send you a sweet "I need you" note.

Psychologists describe these people as giving the message, "Hold me close a little farther away." They can really have you spinning in circles if you don't know what you are doing and often even if you do. They are good at mobilizing other people to help them out of their desperate straits and good at getting themselves into desperate straits. If you feel trapped or obligated in your counseling with someone, that person is quite possibly self-abusing.

The Psychotic Person

A psychotic person lives in an unreal world and believes things to be true that are not true. This person may see, hear, feel, taste, or even smell things others do not. A psychotic person may believe that the CIA is after him, that he is involved in some international or perhaps intergalactic plot, or that he is the Antichrist, Jesus, or Napoleon.

A psychotic person may have what is known as "ideas of reference," that is, ideas that people and events having nothing to do with him are in some way making references to him. Someone who believes that he is getting secret coded messages through the evening news or that a newscaster was referring to him experiences ideas of reference.

It may be fairly obvious that you should not work with these people if you are not sufficiently trained. Often, they need medication to help them, and no amount of talking or listening will make them any better. Some counselors may try to reason them out of their beliefs. Since the problem may not be with reason but with emotions, the arguments are typically wasted.

Some people are less obviously psychotic. These people may make perfect sense and talk rationally about their problems, but after a while they admit to you that they see flashes of blood, violent scenes, dismembered bodies, or snakes. You should refer them too.

A psychotic person can be unintentionally dangerous because the problem is a misconception of what is real. The woman who shoots her son because she genuinely believes that he is in great danger and is trying to protect him is psychotic. The young man who hears voices telling him that to get right with God he must tie his hands and feet and jump into the family pool in order to baptize and cleanse himself is psychotic.

It is essential that counselors have a basic understanding of the nature of psychosis and avoid offering misguided advice to "stop taking pills and start trusting God." If medication is indicated, the consequences of cessation can be tragic. Psychotically disturbed individuals may maim or kill themselves when taken off medication against professional advice. This could be prevented if well-meaning people stay within their own limits.

Work with Professionals

You may have the opportunity to do some supportive counseling with chronic patients. They may have had ongoing mental problems for many years, or they may have actual physical brain dysfunction. In either case, they are people with little human hope of cure.

What they may need from you is not treatment so much as support. Listening and caring is a loving thing to do, and you may really help them feel less lonely and outcast. This may not be an easy thing to do because the chances are that you will hear the same complaints week after week, year after year, but it may still be a ministry and helpful to someone to have you to talk to. Also, if you do this work, you may free a pastor or a psychologist to spend time doing other work.

If you are doing supportive work or any work with someone who is also seeing a professional counselor of any kind, one thing you will definitely want to do is to be in touch with the professional. I suggest that you call if you are a lay counselor or even if you are a pastor. You can say that you have been asked to do some supportive counseling and you are willing to do that if it would help the person cope with life, but you wouldn't want to get in the way or get involved without the professional's knowledge and permission. If you are careful not to misrepresent yourself in any way and you tell the professional that you would be doing only supportive, understanding kinds of things, not giving advice, you will usually get a positive response. Obviously professionals are people too, and some who are incredibly insecure will feel immediately threatened. If this happens to you, please try not to take it personally. You are only responsible to say what your desire is in the best way that you know how to communicate that. You are not responsible for how others react. If you get a positive reaction (and you usually will), you might ask if there is any particular topic to avoid or danger area the professional thinks you should know about.

How to Refer

If you have decided to refer someone, you are doing a loving thing. You are looking out for the best interests of the counselee. Don't let the counselee's reaction cause you to forget that, to feel guilty, or to be manipulated.

Simply tell your counselee that to be the best counselor you know how to be, you believe it is very important to stay within your limits. Not to do that would be wrong and misleading. Say that in the last two sessions you have become increasingly concerned that the counselee may need more than you are able to give in terms of professional training. Then, provide the names of several people you know who have the proper training to cope with the problem. Then hold firm. Once you have decided to refer someone, it is not a good idea to change your mind.

It is also appropriate to ask how the counselee feels. You may suggest that feelings of anger or rejection are not unusual in this situation. Listen to the counselee talk about personal feelings and then end your session.

Graduation

Throughout this chapter I have used the word *referral* on purpose. There is no real termination in therapy. You don't just say, "Good-by, don't come back." You refer counselees to someone else.

But another way for counseling to end, a much happier way, is when the person is feeling better and no longer needs counseling. This is a legitimate graduation. When it is finally graduation time, both counselor and counselee know that it is time. Usually the counselee will ask something like, "How do I know when I am finished?" I usually respond, "Do you feel finished?" You will probably get a good idea from this how the counselee feels.

Of course, there are times when people want to feel better, but they don't want to make any changes or do any growing. These people will terminate themselves, usually by calling on the phone and usually by leaving a message. Or they may cancel an appointment and not call to reschedule. It is fine for you to call and offer to see them again but remember that some will refuse.

I virtually always phase out graduating persons. If they have been doing really well for several weeks, and I have been seeing them on a weekly basis, I might suggest, "This time let's go for two weeks between appointments." Or I might say, "You've been holding together really well with one-week sessions. Let's see how you do with two weeks in between appointments."

Obviously, some people will do well and some won't. If they don't do well, simply go back to weekly appointments. If they do well, repeat the two-week interval a couple of times, then try three weeks or a month. Repeat that for a couple of times, and then suggest a time in three months. Some will say, "No, I'm doing fine now," and that's okay. At the end, let them know that they would be most welcome to call if they find that they are having a problem in the future.

Counselor Support Groups

There is a real need for regular meetings of lay counselors. As a lay counselor, you need a chance to get some new ideas and to share both your successes and problems. This is also a good group to ask for names of professionals if you should need to refer someone. If your church has a lay counseling ministry, the church should also have a counselor support group. If none exists, ask the person in charge to start one. Or you might consider starting one, if that person shows no interest.

You might need to draw from several churches to develop a support group. Ask pastors of other churches for names of lay counselors in their churches, then call them and share the idea. This is virgin territory so your options are wide open. You are limited only by your creativity and energy, but try to get people together so that you don't have to function in this ministry alone.

Counselor Burn-Out

Counselor burn-out is not usually a major problem with the lay counselor who does only a few hours of counseling each week. With a professional, who may spend thirty to thirty-five hours a week listening to people relate their problems, it can be a significant emotional drain, and counselor burn-out is often the result.

The symptoms of burn-out sound a lot like those of depression: low mood, lethargy, lack of excitement in the work, and possibly sleep disturbance. I always know when I have too high a stress level because I have trouble getting to sleep or I wake up very early in the morning and cannot get back to sleep. Your symptoms may vary, but they will often be in the same general category.

The surest cause for counselor burn-out is simply carrying more than you can handle. You may be counseling too many hours a week, or you may be carrying too much responsibility for someone else's life. Remember, all you can do is offer to help. Each counselee must learn individual responsibility.

Let's imagine that you and I live in the same apartment building. Let's say we both had cable TV, both with remote controls. What if you somehow got the idea that I was watching the Playboy channel and you decided that you didn't want me to do that, so you spent a whole evening pushing the buttons on your remote control trying to change my station?

It simply wouldn't work, would it? Your remote control changes only your channels and mine changes only mine. All you would get for your efforts is a sore finger from pushing buttons all night long and maybe a burned-out control. If you try to push other people's buttons in counseling, you will get burned-out too. It simply doesn't work. Forcing other people's lives is not helpful. It is not right or biblical. People won't take the responsibility for themselves if you are going to carry that responsibility for them. Watch out for this genuine hazard of becoming too involved in other people's lives.

Unrealistic Expectations

It is important that you avoid having unrealistic expectations about yourself as a counselor. Listening, caring, and understanding require a lot of time and effort, and they are very helpful. But think of yourself as a helper, not a healer. Don't think of yourself as a lifeguard, pulling up drowning people and holding their heads above water. It is more like you are saying to someone, "I know that's a scary situation to be in, but I think if you will try to notice what you are doing there and remember what you have learned, you can probably swim or at least float." Counseling can be a difficult though rewarding ministry. If you don't keep your own feet on the ground, you too may sink and require counseling.

Only God is without limits. All counselors have limits, and the most well-trained, most professional counselors acknowledge these limits. You should almost certainly refer suicidal, self-abusing, psychotic, and law-breaking counselees to a professional. In addition, you will likely have certain specific categories of people or problems you would prefer not to counsel. Finally, you should be in a support group if possible and ask for help and supervision when necessary.

7

Premarital Counseling

We live in an age when the institution of marriage has fallen on hard times. It is estimated that forty-five out of one hundred first-time marriages end in divorce. To put this into everyday language, it is estimated that 1,986 couples divorce every day. In February 1980, *Newsweek* did a cover story on this subject and noted that there are 12 million children under eighteen whose parents are divorced and that 45 percent of children born in any given year will live with only one of their parents before age eighteen.

Before I began this book, I conducted a survey with pastors and asked them what they thought should be included in a book on counseling. One of the things that was mentioned by almost everyone was premarital counseling. In a time when marriage seems to be so risky, we need to do everything we can to help young couples build their married lives on a sound foundation.

The Purpose of Premarital Counseling

Most people think the purpose of premarital counseling is obvious, but there is a surprising diversity in what they think that obvious answer is. Some say the purpose is to prepare a couple for marriage. Some say it is to prepare and plan the wedding ceremony. Others say it is for the pastor to decide whether he is going to perform the marriage. Still others say it is to help ensure that the couple stays married. I believe several of these issues are involved, but if you do any premarital counseling, you will need to decide your goals and objectives before you set up your methodology.

A couple will need to spend at least an hour with someone from the church going over arrangements for the ceremony. They may discuss the actual physical setup of the sanctuary—where the vows will be exchanged, where the flowers will go, where the musicians will be, and so on. They may also discuss the reception, if that is to be at the church. The pastor need not be involved in all these arrangements. Many churches have someone in charge of coordinating this sort of thing.

The pastor and the couple usually spend some time together planning the ceremony. Some pastors still are heavily involved in these plans. Some don't plan it because they do exactly the same ceremony they have always done. In some cases the bride shows up and the pastor runs everything, telling everyone where to stand and what to say and do. In some cases the pastor shows up and the bride tells him where to stand and what to say and do. The instances when the couple plan their own ceremony and write their own vows to reflect their own personality and style are definitely becoming more frequent. If this is what the couple want, they need to clarify that with the pastor early on, along with who will get the organist, who will communicate with the janitor, who will run the rehearsal, and so on.

Newlywed Counseling

By the time a couple has publicly announced their engagement, there are only two chances that a pastor or a counselor can talk them out of getting married—slim and none. Even though most pastors require some kind of premarital counseling, most who have been doing counseling for more than ten years wonder aloud if the starry-eyed couple has heard a word they say.

Because of this, some older pastors are opting for a fairly brief time of premarital counseling, perhaps only two sessions; then they ask the couple to return for counseling sessions after they are married. If I were to use this method, I would require a couple to sign a contract promising to come for counseling sessions after they have been married three months, six months, and one year. (If I were pastoring a church, I think I would have every couple sign a contract agreeing to pay five hundred dollars for the wedding to the church unless they returned for all three newlywed checkups, in which case the entire debt would be forgiven.) These newlywed sessions would focus primarily on communications skills and conflict resolution.

I believe that newlywed counseling sessions will become the norm in the future to help newlyweds establish healthy patterns and to help prevent problems. After several months of marriage, the couple have learned that life is not always a honeymoon. They may be finally motivated to listen and learn how to communicate truthfully and lovingly.

The Shorter Approach

In the approach to premarital counseling that is limited to two or three sessions with the pastor, several basic areas should be covered. The couple should talk about children and family plans. If they have already discussed this on their own, all the better. But the counselor should ask what they have specifically decided, not just whether they have discussed it. Family plans include birth control, size of family, and when they would like to start a family. How do they feel about the wife working? What did they like or dislike about the way their parents raised and disciplined them? If they each have very strong feelings in this area or one of them has had some bad experiences growing up, these points should be discussed.

The couple should discuss relationships with in-laws. Where will they live? How will they relate to their parents? How often will they call or visit? Will they still be under their parents' authority after they are married? Also, holiday visits should be discussed and possibly a plan worked out.

Finances should be discussed. A basic budget should be worked out. Who will pay the bills? Who will physically write the checks? Are they going to live on one income or two? Some biblical teaching about debt is important, and how they both feel about debt and credit cards should be discussed.

There are occasions when sex should be discussed, but frankly, this is less an issue now than it was fifty years ago. Even if both partners are virgins, they are probably not ill-informed, but the subject should be touched upon anyway.

An Alternative to the Traditional Approach

In a small church, the pastor may feel that he has ample opportunity to meet and know every engaged couple. In medium-sized and larger-sized churches, however, there is usually less familiarity with the couple preparing to be married. This creates difficulties in evaluating the potential for a healthy relationship and in being aware of potential problems. Along with this, the many duties of the pastoral staff make it impossible for them to meet all need. It is not really a biblical approach to say that pastors are to do all the ministry: pastors are to equip the saints for the work of the ministry. I would like to propose, therefore, a premarriage ministry in the church. This ministry would provide the opportunity to utilize trained and qualified lay counselors for the work alongside or under the supervision of the professional pastoral staff.

I am indebted to Omar Zook, a Christian layman and qualified counselor, who has done much of the work in setting up a pilot program in my former church, the Evangelical Free Church of Hershey. Many of the thoughts and words in the next few pages are his and are used with his permission. Lay counselors do much of the training and counseling of couples planning to be married. I think this church of about two thousand people has come up with a biblical approach to meeting this need. And it makes a lot more sense than expecting pastors to counsel one hundred couples a year. I hope that many people will consider adding such a ministry to their churches.

Objectives

   I. Encourage and establish marital relationships that are effective, fulfilling, and lasting.

  II. Evaluate relationships for problems that would hinder or detract from a healthy marriage and provide appropriate guidance as indicated.

III. Enable couples to establish a positive, wholesome marital foundation upon which to build their homes.

IV. Cultivate and foster a reciprocal, mutually enriching church-home interrelationship. The church can help equip couples for wholesome marital and family living, and the couples, in turn, can contribute to the well-being of the church body.

  V. Provide ongoing training and supervision of couples who do the counseling.

Design

I. Training.

   A. Select qualified couples to assist in providing pre-marriage counseling. Qualifications include having a healthy, Christian marriage, being able to effectively relate to others, to identify signs of health and pathology and to provide assistance as indicated.

B. Have selected couples complete the premarriage course to become familiarized with the course material.

C. Through ongoing supervision by pastor or other trained professionals, provide needed assistance and foster continued development of skills.

II. Couples desiring to be married will contact the pastoral staff and then be referred for premarriage counseling, assuming the pastoral staff and/or elder board agrees to marry them. If concern arises during the course about whether counseling regarding the appropriateness of the marriage should take place, this shall be shared with the pastoral staff, and the final decision will rest with them and/or the elder board.

III. Consultation will be made with the pastoral team to determine which couple is best suited to provide counseling for a given couple.

IV. The premarriage counseling course will consist of five premarriage sessions and one newlywed session, as outlined here. The number of sessions may be altered in the event a couple needs additional work in a given area.

Before First Session

I. Meet with the couple informally to become acquainted and to give material for Taylor-Johnson Temperament Analysis (T-JTA, see Appendix) and homework questions for first session. Couple doing the counseling should take the initiative in arranging this meeting.

II. Complete the T-JTA.
III. Complete the following questions:
   A. What is your definition of *marriage*?
   B. How were feelings of love, warmth, and tenderness shown in your home as you were growing up? How would you like feelings of love, warmth, and tenderness shown in public and in your home after you marry?
   C. How have your attitudes toward marriage been influenced? Who influenced them?
   D. What fears do you have about marriage?
IV. The pastoral staff and/or lay counselors will want to compile a bibliography of readings, some of which may be suggested and some required for all couples. In addition, further reading may be added to supplement a particular couple's weak areas.

Session One

I. Establish ground rules.
   A. There is nothing that cannot be discussed in these sessions. Confidentiality will be maintained.
   B. Emphasize the importance of completing homework assignments.
   C. Stress the need for honesty with each other.
II. Review couple's definitions of marriage (then hand out these definitions and review).
   A. A covenant made under God in the presence of fellow members of the Christian family.
   B. Created by God as a means of companionship, love, and intimacy to be experienced and expressed.
   C. An unconditional love commitment of two imperfect people—does not demand perfection.
   D. A total commitment of two people to Jesus Christ

and to each other; a partnership of mutual subordination.

E. Like a solvent—a freeing up of the man and woman to be themselves and become all that God intends for them to become.

F. A refining process—becoming more aware of rough edges. Complexities of life will increase because two people are involved instead of one. God will allow trials and pressures to come—the attitude toward them will be all important.

III. Discuss dating background.
   A. How long have they dated?
   B. What kinds of dates have they had?
   C. What kinds of things do they enjoy doing together?

IV. Explore extent of their preparation for marriage. Have they:
   A. Read any books?
   B. Taken any classes?
   C. Been to any seminars?

V. Talk about how attitudes toward marriage have been influenced and who influenced them.

VI. What fears are there about marriage? Give reassurance about many couples having fears.

VII. Explore couple's Christian beliefs.
   A. Have each share personal beliefs.
   B. Ask following questions:
      1. How important is God to each of them?
      2. How long have they been affiliated with a church?
      3. What church background do they have?
   C. Encourage couple to begin devotions together on a regular basis and determine which verses they want to build their marriage upon.

    D. Have the couple think about a style of devotional life that is meaningful to them.

VIII. Explore couple's definition of love.

    A. Have each answer, "Why do you feel you are in love with this particular person?"

    B. Hand out and review the following definitions.

        1. Real love—an unconditional commitment to an imperfect person.

        2. A person is in love with another individual when meeting the emotional needs of that person becomes an emotional need of his/her own life.

        3. Study 1 Corinthians 13.

        4. To really love another person means to love self also.

        5. Share the difference between the feeling of being "in love," which can come and go, and the decision or commitment to love, which is committing one's self to the other's greatest good.

IX. Homework assignment (this assignment is due at the beginning of the third session).

    A. Obtain feelings and/or feedback from parents regarding the marriage, if couple has not done so already.

        1. If couple has approached both sets of parents, discuss each parent's reaction. If any negative reaction was given, carefully evaluate it.

        2. If couple has not approached parents, pursue their plan for doing so. Ask how they feel about the importance of obtaining parental blessing for their marriage.

    B. Have each individual write answers to the following:

    1. The ways in which my needs can best be met by my spouse-to-be are...

    2. These are the ways in which I will attempt to meet the needs of my spouse in these same three areas...

C. Write twelve to fifteen reasons why you want to marry this person.

D. Describe the goals you have for your marriage. (If necessary, explain that a goal is the direction or purpose of the marriage or what a person wants the marriage to accomplish.)

E. Write a paragraph on what you are bringing to this marriage that will make it work.

Session Two

I. Meet with each individual separately and review results of the T-JTA. Have each spouse of counseling couple meet individual of same sex of engaged couple. Review results only of individual with whom you are meeting—the individual's own score and the score reflecting perceptions of the other person. Discuss any questions and/or concerns.

II. Meet with the couple together to review results of the T-JTA.

A. Begin by showing the man's profile to the woman and discussing potential problems. Then show the woman's to the man. Finally show them how they see each other. Discuss any questions as to how they see themselves or each other.

B. Focus on personality differences and the areas that may require possible adjustment.

C. Focus on ways they are alike. Sometimes being too alike can cause difficulties.

III. Is couple following through with devotional life and prayer time together?

IV. Is couple reading books assigned prior to the first session? How far are they along?

V. Homework assignment. Complete Bible study sheet on marriage prepared by pastor or lay leader.

Session Three

I. Review homework questions from first session.

A. When reviewing reasons why they want to marry, look for balance between what person receives for self and also what will be given to the other person.

B. For question, What are you bringing to this marriage that will make it work? have couple:

1. Name the personal characteristics each possesses that will build up a marriage.

2. List qualities each one wishes to change about mate. How do they propose to effect changes? Discuss: Is changing each other a good idea? Is it possible? Remind them that they fell in love with each other as they are now. What would happen to the love if they were successful in changing each other? Remind them that they are getting a whole package, with strengths and weaknesses. They have the option of not marrying, but the package comes as designed. There are no user serviceable parts. They buy the whole thing as is or leave it in the store.

II. Sexual involvement.

A. Explore extent of sexual involvement:

1. To what extent have they expressed affection to each other?

2. Have they agreed upon the limit to which they will go in expressing affection to each other?

3. Are they comfortable with that limit?

B. Obtain commitment to abstain from sexual rela-

tions. Avoids guilt and allows for clearer assessment of how much relationship is based on physical attraction. Biblical instruction is clear: 1 Thessalonians 4:3; Acts 15:29; 1 Corinthians 6:15; 10:8; Ephesians 5:3; Colossians 3:5.
C. Initiate opportunity for forgiveness, if appropriate.

III. Family.
Consider each partner's individual family background:
A. Where each lived?
B. Type of home?
C. What were parents like?
D. How large a family?
E. What was family like?
F. Parents' occupations?
G. Individual relationships within the family?
H. Parents' physical and mental health?
I. How were disagreements handled?
J. How were decisions made?
K. How were finances handled?
L. Was there always enough money?

IV. Communication.
A. Read Ephesians 4:15 about speaking the truth in love. Discuss: What is communicating the truth without love? What is trying to be loving without being truthful? What happens when these things are done?
B. Try some examples of speaking the truth in love.
1. How can you say, "You need to take a shower" in the speaking-the-truth-in-love method?
2. How can you say, "I am angry about what you did at the party," in the speaking-the-truth-in-love method?

V. Homework assignment.

A. Each member of the couple should try three times to speak the truth in love and write down what was said and how it worked.

B. Read *Intended for Pleasure* by Ed and Gaye Wheat, Chapters 1–5.

C. Discuss desires and preferences they each have for the first night of the honeymoon.

D. Is the couple reading the assigned books from the first session?

Session Four

I. Discuss sexual relationship.

A. Should have read *Intended for Pleasure* by Ed and Gaye Wheat. Discuss any questions or issues raised by this.

B. Review scriptural view of sex. God created sex for several purposes: procreation, pleasure, and means of closeness and intimacy.

C. Review specific details of sexual relationship (if there are questions).

D. Encourage couple to talk openly and freely in their marriage about their sexual relationship. They should explore together ways they can mutually receive the most enjoyment from their sexual relationship.

Explain:

1. There is a tuning process which happens. Sometimes sexual fulfillment takes time to reach.

2. Flexibility and freedom regarding time and place should be exercised.

3. Point out importance of cleanliness due to body odors, which can inhibit sexual responsiveness or excitement.

4. Talk frankly and openly to the man about the

97

need to be sensitive to little things that are important to the woman—showing affection regardless of whether or not it pertains to sexual involvement. Emphasize differences in time for man and woman to reach climax.

II. Honeymoon.

Find out whether homework question was completed and discuss any questions the couple may have. Encourage them to maintain a sense of humor as they will likely make some mistakes.

III. Children.

A. Have they discussed children? How many they want, when they want to start a family, and so on.

B. What are their ideas of discipline and child rearing?

C. What expectations do they have of each other? Is rearing the children to be the woman's job or will they share? How will they share?

D. Recommend *How to Really Love Your Child* by Ross Campbell.

E. An excellent way to prepare for parenthood is to volunteer time in a church nursery! Discuss time for doing this.

IV. In-Laws.

A. Review feelings and/or feedback from parents if this has not been done earlier.

B. Questions to discuss:

1. What is your attitude toward your parents and your future in-laws?

2. How close will you live to them? Do you feel it would be possible to live a thousand miles away from your parents?

3. How do you anticipate dealing with your par-

ents after marriage? How much time will you want to spend with them? How often will you visit?

4. Are you dependent on them financially?

C. Guidelines for dealing with in-laws:

1. Treat them just like you would a friend. If they give advice, treat it like advice from a friend. If it is good advice, follow it. If it is not good, graciously accept it and lay it aside.

2. Look for their good points.

3. Get to know them as much as possible.

4. Accept them as they are. Don't try to change them.

5. See them as part of the family.

V. Homework assignment.

A. Complete first-year budget.

B. Is couple consistently having devotions together?

C. Is couple reading assigned books from first session?

Session Five

I. Emotional needs.

A. How do you want your spouse to respond to you when you cry?

B. After you are married, how do you think you will feel about your spouse relating to members of the opposite sex? At work? Friendships? You will likely notice members of the opposite sex and may even be attracted to them. How will you handle this?

C. How much praise do you feel you need? How will you want it expressed?

D. What activities will you want to continue separately after you are married? What activities together? It is important to do things together but allow space to do things separately too.

II. Finances.
  A. Review first-year budget.
  B. Discuss following questions:
      1. How realistic is couple's idea of what it takes to live today?
      2. Will couple build life-style around one paycheck or two (if both are working)?
      3. How much experience has couple had dealing with money?
      4. Who will be responsible for handling finances after they are married?
      5. How do they plan to handle money matters?
          a) It is important that both become aware of their finances and how they are being handled.
          b) Is there flexibility in adjusting budget if needed?
  C. Review three basic principles regarding finances:
      1. All money brought in should be regarded as "family" money, with each person informed of its source and destination.
      2. Money should be used based on mutual discussion and agreement.
      3. Each person should receive a small amount for personal use without having to account for it.

III. Review couple's spiritual life together.
  A. Are they maintaining devotional and prayer time together?
  B. How do they feel about it?
  C. What Bible verses did they select to build their marriage upon?

IV. Schedule newlywed visit approximately three months past the date of marriage.

    V. Present gift (a book is often a good idea).

    VI. Closing comments.

First Newlywed Session

Review following areas:

    I. Get general feeling about the marriage.

       A. Is it what they expected?

       B. What surprises, if any, have occurred?

       C. Have any major changes occurred? A new job, a move, are they expecting a child?

       D. How is each contributing to the well-being of the marriage?

    II. Are they maintaining the goals they had for the marriage?

    III. Relationship with parents.

    IV. Spiritual relationship.

       A. Are they maintaining church involvement?

       B. Do they take time for devotionals together?

    V. Life-style.

       A. Are they giving each other quality time?

       B. Are they satisfied with each other's schedule?

    VI. Communication.

       A. Have there been major conflicts or disagreements? How have they handled them?

       B. Does each express himself/herself openly enough? Too openly?

    VII. Sexual adjustment.

       A. Are they satisfied with their sexual adjustment?

       B. Is affection shown routinely aside from intercourse?

    VIII. Finances.

       A. Are they following a budget successfully?

       B. Have they been in agreement with the budget?

The Bible clearly talks about older people in the church being leaders and guides for younger people. I hope that the lay counseling couple will be available to encourage the newlyweds and will be able to keep in contact with them. It would be a good idea for the counseling couple to get together with the newlyweds in a social setting, take them out to dinner or invite them over some evening, if that is possible. This would be helpful before and particularly after the marriage. It is important that each church and each program add to or adapt these general ideas and tailor them for the needs of the particular church.

In this chapter, I have suggested a new format for a comprehensive premarital counseling program developed by Omar Zook. I also suggested that newlywed counseling may be a far more effective use of time and energy than traditional premarital counseling programs. Each church and each pastor should adapt and develop a premarital program that will suit their own philosophy and meet the needs of the newlyweds.

The Most Common Marriage Problems

Virtually all marital problems occur in one of seven areas. If the counselor has a grasp of general counseling principles (such as those set forth in this book) and knowledge of these areas (as well as dependence on God's leading), marriage counseling need not be such a mystery.

In this chapter I will discuss the four "major" problem areas of marriage, which make up approximately 80 percent of the marital problems counselors encounter. To take a somewhat positive approach to this subject, I have identified some principles that can help couples avoid problems in these specific areas. If a counselor can guide couples to a healthy position in relation to these principles, the counseling is usually successful.

In the next chapter I will discuss the three "minor" problem areas. These can be just as serious and can cause just as much trouble for a couple as the major areas, but a counselor has to deal with them less often. I will also discuss some general marriage counseling issues and techniques.

Communication

Let's begin with the easiest principle to recognize and to teach in marriage counseling. It is also an easy principle for the counselees to understand, although it certainly takes practice and effort to move from the level of understanding to the level of changed behavior.

The principle comes from Ephesians 4:15, that is, we are to speak the truth in love. Two basic problems can arise from failure to follow this principle. The first is to speak what we perceive as the truth in an unloving way. The second is to say what we feel is the "loving" thing without truth.

A lot of harsh, damaging statements are made in marriage counseling sessions. These are a result of someone saying the truth as it is perceived (it very well may not be the actual truth), but with no real attempt to communicate that "truth" in a loving way. When an angry husband says, "She is fat. She won't take care of herself. The idea of going to bed with her is disgusting to me. And she is a lousy housekeeper," he is stating his version of the truth without love.

When a counselee makes this kind of explosive, angry, and frankly destructive statement and you are aware that one of the basic principles is being violated, that is not necessarily the signal for you to interrupt the eruption and preach a little sermon on "talking nice." Although some teaching is involved in counseling, it is not a good idea to interrupt a counselee early in the counseling process. It is especially not a good idea to interrupt with the message, "Don't be angry." Since the counselee is being honest with you about what he feels, you need to listen to him to find out how he perceives things.

After he finishes expressing his opinion, you might ask him how he thinks his wife is feeling right now, or you might ask her how she is feeling. The counseling sessions are the times to teach people how to notice their feelings and how to express them in a simple, direct, and loving way. So, when you ask a counselee, "What are you feeling right now?" or "I am wondering what you were feeling when you heard him say these things?" make sure you get an answer to your question. Fairly often, a counselee won't be talking about emotions at all but will simply launch into a counterattack of some kind, such as, "Why should I take care of myself the way he treats me?"

Bring the counselee back on course with something like this. "You have asked me a question, but I want you to tell me how you feel when he says these things about you."

Even at this point, the counselee, especially in early sessions, may not get the idea and may answer with a slightly disguised attack, such as, "Well, I feel that he shouldn't talk to me that way." Here is a way to handle this problem.

COUNSELOR. "He shouldn't talk to me that way" is not the name of an emotion. What emotion happens inside of you when your husband says you are disgusting?

WIFE. It hurts. I feel like he doesn't love me.

COUNSELOR. You feel hurt and unloved. [*Notice I have rephrased her statement—"like he doesn't love me," which is not quite an emotion, to "unloved," which is.*]

At this point I would get her to communicate the truth in love to him. I would say, "Why don't you look right at him and tell him you feel hurt and unloved?" (Expect the couple to be uncomfortable with this. Most couples who come for counseling simply don't know how to speak the truth about their feelings in a simple, brief, nonattacking, "I feel" statement.) Even when you suggest that she say, "I feel hurt and unloved," frequently she won't do that but will say, "He's right" or "I do." Once again, you may have to guide her into how to do it right. I would say, "Tell him the whole sentence." Finally, she will look up briefly at her spouse and say, "I feel hurt and unloved when you say that." (Notice how brief this statement is. In truthful, loving communication, briefer is better.)

You can now turn to the angry, disgusted husband, who has just gotten a glimpse of a hurt, nonattacking wife. Nine times out of ten you will see that he has already softened somewhat. To get a response from him I would turn to him and say, "Bob, she says when you call her fat and disgusting she feels hurt and unloved."

He might say something like, "Well, I am sorry, but I get so frustrated. She has always known that weight and appearance are important things to me."

COUNSELOR. Why don't you tell *her*?
BOB. [*He looks at her.*] Well, they are.
COUNSELOR. Why don't you say the whole sentence?
BOB. Weight and appearance are important things to me.
COUNSELOR. Did you notice you left out part of your sentence?
BOB. [*Blank look. He has no idea what I am talking about.*]
COUNSELOR. I thought I heard you say, "I'm sorry, but I get so frustrated."
BOB. Oh, yeah.
COUNSELOR. Bob, I am sure you are not aware of it, but you very often leave out the "I" messages, the "I am sorries," the personal emotions, the warmth, when you talk to Betty. She needs that warm part of you, and I wonder if there would be a way that you could express your feelings, your disappointments, in a way that still had some love in it, so they wouldn't be quite so hurtful?

Love without Truth

While you, the counselor, are more likely to see the truth-without-love problem in a counseling session, the love-without-truth problem is often the primary reason why the couple is seeking help. What is love without truth? Well, here again the "love" has to be in quotes. It is not really loving to hold in the truth, but many people think it is. Many people will not say that they are angry or hurt or that they are not having their needs met, because they are trying to avoid the trouble that they think would come with being truthful.

Years ago a friend of mine was newly married. His wife was a farm girl and was used to the family having a big breakfast, but he was raised in the city and couldn't stomach anything but coffee before 10:00 in the morning. To make matters worse, he had a job as a milkman while he was working his way through college. For the first month of marriage, she got up at 4:00 A.M. to make him a big breakfast, which he dutifully ate, then he got in the car, drove a half-block from the house, and promptly lost his entire breakfast on the street. This went on for four weeks before he risked being truthful with her. It seems silly, doesn't it, but the lack of truthful expression is a significant marriage problem.

Many people with good motivation simply bury or hold in their irritations or hurts rather than risk injuring the other person or the relationship. I often tell couples that every unexpressed negative emotion is another brick in the wall between them. If the wall is allowed to get high enough, it seems impossible to see the other person anymore or to get any love through it.

When you are seeing a couple for counseling and one of them remains unwilling to work on the relationship, in almost every case another man or woman is involved or that person has held in negative feelings for years, trying to "keep the peace" and now the wall is too high to jump over. In fact, many of you may find that the problems of the wall of unexpressed emotions and the other man/woman often occur together. Of the two, I believe the other man/woman is the easier problem to deal with, because when someone can't see through the wall of unexpressed negative emotion and can't get any love through that wall, little motivation will remain to work on the relationship. It is in this context and into this relationship that the other man/woman often enters.

The treatment is to explain the wall and the importance of keeping the lines of communication uncluttered. Then get the couple to talk, bringing out the emotional content and teaching them how to do it.

PAUL. I am sorry we are late. Kathryn didn't have the kids ready for the baby-sitter.

COUNSELOR. That sounds like she may have made you angry.

PAUL. Oh no, I'm not angry. I was just explaining.

COUNSELOR. Being on time is pretty important to you?

PAUL. Yes, very. I don't know why. I guess I think it's rude to be late.

COUNSELOR. And you felt Kathryn was making you be rude by being late?

PAUL. It's not important. I don't know why we are talking about it. I just felt like she had all morning to get herself and the two kids ready, and I don't understand why she couldn't do that.

COUNSELOR. You don't have any feelings about it. Your interest is merely intellectual curiosity about why this happened.

PAUL. [Silence.]

COUNSELOR. Do I remember you saying you were sorry when you came in? That sounds like an emotion.

PAUL. Okay, okay. I was just a little bit frustrated. But I think we should be using this time to resolve some of the "important" issues we came here to talk about.

COUNSELOR. You'd like us to quit talking about emotions and get down to the really important stuff.

PAUL. [Silence.]

COUNSELOR. I don't think you are aware of this, but I doubt that any issue is more important in your relationship than how you express your emotions with each other. If that is going well, many of these so-called important issues on your list will be taken care of automatically. Would it be so terrible to admit you were annoyed by being late? She knows it anyway. She can tell by your tone of voice and your whole manner.

In this case, as in many others, when the truth was not expressed directly (where it can be consciously controlled and therefore loving, clear, and brief), it comes out indirectly through things like tone of voice and body language. The sooner the emotional truth can be expressed (or if you prefer "confessed") in a loving way, the sooner it is resolved and the relationship is healed and protected.

"You've Got to Be Different"

If the first principle to remember is speaking the truth in love, the second is unconditional acceptance. Unconditional acceptance means that one spouse doesn't try to change the other. It means *not* saying, "You've got to be different." Romans 5:8 says that God loved us "while we were still sinners." He loved (and still loves) us perfectly. He didn't demand that we first "get holy"; He loved us where we were. True, because of His unconditional love, we respond by changing, but the love happens first.

The same is true in counseling. Wouldn't it be foolish for a counselor to say to a counselee, "First, you get your act together, and then I will accept you for counseling"? On the other hand, I have seen people make great strides in their personal growth and mental health after they have seen me demonstrate God's unconditional love by accepting them as they were.

The importance of the counselor's acceptance of the counselee is demonstrated in this story. A woman with depression and very low self-image was hospitalized, but she remained desperate even there. One night she got a piece of glass and cut herself forty to fifty times on each arm. She carved several words, including *God* and *help,* on her arms. She assumed that her doctor would be very angry when he found what she had done. She feared he would say he didn't want to treat her any more.

His reaction to her self-abuse was very much the opposite, however. He told her she was not in trouble with him and added, "You must have been feeling very pained and desperate." That woman now attributes her turnaround in therapy to the day when she thought she had really blown it and found out, much to her surprise, that she was still acceptable.

The unconditional acceptance principle is vitally necessary in a happy marriage and must therefore be taught in marriage counseling. How is this accomplished? First, I think it is taught indirectly by the counselor's modeling it to the couple. Second, it is taught directly (and briefly) by the counselor as something that is godly and important. Third, it is taught by helping counselees understand that each of them is responsible for their own emotions.

If Cindy is angry at Charlie because he always leaves his shoes and socks in the middle of the living room floor, the counseling session could focus on why Charlie leaves his shoes out when he knows it bothers Cindy. But a much more productive discussion would involve why it makes Cindy angry and how she deals with her anger. Getting Charlie to pick up his shoes and socks is changing only behavior. Charlie is still Charlie, and there will always be a list of things Charlie does that Cindy doesn't understand. Marriage counseling is much more productive when time is spent not resolving specific conflicts (such as picking up or not picking up your shoes) but rather teaching each spouse how to resolve personal conflicts. This comes as each person admits, "The only part of the problem I can fix is me, and there is no use wasting energy trying to change the other person."

LUKE. She cries at the drop of a hat. I can't say anything to her without her crying. She is not interested in anything I like. If I am five minutes late, she starts to worry. I never saw anybody who comes up with more things to worry about.

MARIE. He doesn't care about anything unless it has shoulder pads or shin guards. I plan a nice romantic dinner, and all he can say is, "No potatoes?" Why can't he dress up when we go out? My friends must think I am married to a farmer.

Counseling during the early stages of marriage almost exclusively has something to do with these "you've got to be different" comments. The objective, essentially, is for both spouses to recognize that when they got married, they bought the whole package, strengths and weaknesses. A husband can focus on his wife's weaknesses if he wants, but that doesn't mean she will change. Usually through counseling, the husband's attitude toward his wife, rather than her behavior, would change. Once the husband gives up trying to get his wife to change and returns to an accepting way of loving her (or perhaps goes on to a new stage in accepting her), within the context of a loving, accepting relationship she may make many of the changes he was simply unable to "get her to" make before. Of course, the same principle is true for wives trying to change husbands.

That phrase "get him (or her) to" is one to watch out for. When one person is trying to get another person to do something, the individual taking responsibility has no real control and frustration is the most likely outcome. Children may be an exception here, but with adults, ultimately, no one can "get" someone else to do something for very long.

Continual Investment of Affections

The third principle is that of continual investment of affections. This principle applies to two of the primary reasons why people come for marriage counseling, "I am not in love anymore" and "the other man/woman."

Revelation 2:4 says to the church at Ephesus that it had left its "first love." Likewise, the church at Laodicea is referred to as no longer hot or cold but simply lukewarm (see Rev. 3:16). Both conditions are described as being wrong. While it is certainly true that these verses describe churches, the relationship of Christ and the church is consistently compared to that of husbands and wives. The Bible seems to teach in these verses that there is a tendency for relationships to deteriorate. Let's look at why that is and what to do about it.

A part of your heart is designed to be given away. If that part of your heart is in your possession, it will be constantly "trying out" people you meet of the opposite sex, looking for someone who fits or matches you emotionally. There is nothing wrong with this system. I believe it is the way God made human beings.

When two people meet, date, and fall in love, that "in love" part of the heart is gradually being invested in the loved one. There is no real effort involved. They just spend time together listening, talking, getting to know each other, caring, and to a great extent just playing. Most couples did not fall in love while involved in some deep philosophical discussion. Rather, they were on a hayride, at a basketball game, or on a picnic. The first time you give your heart away to a particular person, you do so effortlessly, enjoyably, and usually gradually.

But there is a problem. I suppose it is because of the Fall and the fact that we are all basically selfish people. For whatever reason, when you give your heart away, there is something like a rubber band attached to it. This means that after a while (generally a period of years for most people), without any conscious decision on your part, that "in love" part of your heart snaps back and is once again in your possession.

This is a dangerous, vulnerable time. Because your heart is designed to find someone to fit, it will begin the search immediately. The only indication you might have that your heart is back in your possession might be that you notice yourself mentally "trying out" people, perhaps fantasizing about what life would be like with them.

Ideally, in a healthy marriage, the partners spend enough "playtime" together, dating, listening, talking, laughing, basically doing the same things they did when they fell in love the first time. If they do this, they will fall in love again and again. This is virtually as scientific and predictable as when hydrogen and oxygen are put together in the correct ratio and water is made. But if the partners have stopped doing the things they did when they fell in love the first time, if they don't talk, don't laugh, don't listen, don't play, and don't accept each other, how can they reinvest their affections?

If you want your marriage to remain healthy, you must spend enough regular, positive playtime alone together. I am not talking about sex here. That playtime is fine, but not nearly sufficient. I know many couples with terrible relationships who claim that the only good thing about their marriage is sex. Spouses need positive, enjoyable time together not related to sex and not with other people. I suggest that you, as a Christian worker and example, adopt this policy for your own marriage and then teach it to others.

If a couple comes to you and says, "We are not in love anymore," explain how the investment of affections works. Ask them if they will commit themselves to taking daily walks, going out on dates, and basically repeating the emotional conditions that existed when they fell in love the first time.

What happens in a situation where the emotions have been invested in another man or woman? It is not enough in these cases to have the married couple spend time together. A man can't give away what he doesn't have, and if he has given away his heart, he will have to get it back before he can reinvest it in his wife.

Taking back your heart, on purpose, is a painful process. In a way it is both noble and courageous for the wife, who has fallen in love with another man, to decide to take back her heart and reinvest it in her husband just because she knows it is the right thing to do. Why noble and courageous? Emotionally she is voluntarily going through the same process of retrieving her heart as she would have had to go through if her husband suddenly divorced her to marry his girlfriend. Breaking off a loving relationship, whether you decide to do it or whether the other party decides to do it, is still painful, difficult, and gradual. It is emotional divorce.

From the moment a married man or woman invests affection in someone outside the marriage relationship, pain is inevitable. The only remaining questions are, How many people will get hurt? and Which people? The pain always happens. It is often good to remind counselors that it is not the putting right of things that caused the pain but the misplacing of affections in the first place.

Before agreeing to counsel with a couple that has gone through the experience of the other man/woman, many counselors require that the involved partner have no further contact with the third party. I think there is some wisdom in this position because marriage counseling is pretty well wasted if one of the partners has an extra partner on the side. In such cases, I have seen the people individually to help them face and make a decision as to which direction they will choose. This is often helpful, but marriage counseling, before the last good-by to the other party, may not be helpful.

It is important for you, the counselor, to maintain an understanding, nonjudgmental position. Most "involved" people didn't do so with malice or forethought. They got involved a little bit at a time. Also, a counselor who pushes too hard for a decision will lose the couple altogether, or the counselee may simply lie and tell the counselor what is expected.

Who's on First?

I have had some difficulty trying to put this fourth principle into a simple statement because so many things seem to be involved. But I'll call this principle "power for others." It includes the issues of meeting needs, being a servant, and caring for yourself. In other words, this is the "who is responsible for what" principle.

In Philippians 2:7 we are told that Christ became a servant and did whatever was necessary to meet our needs. We are told in Ephesians 5:25 that husbands are to wives as Christ is to the church, that is, its servant Messiah, One who leads by meeting needs. Wives are told in Ephesians 5:22 and 24 to submit themselves to their husbands. They are told to *submit* themselves because the very word means that it is something that people can do only for themselves. I can't "submit" someone else. It is done from within, voluntarily. And finally, in case there was any doubt, Ephesians 5:21 says husbands and wives should submit to each other.

A summary of all this would be to say that each spouse is responsible to try to meet the needs of the other. This is true and basic to good marriage, but it is not everything.

Each of us has the basic need to make personal decisions and develop an identity as an individual, so the most the spouse could do to meet this need would be to offer support and encouragement. A husband can't develop an identity for his wife. If he tried, he would develop not her identity but his identity. I believe there are also times and ways in which we need to be responsible for ourselves.

Another responsibility of a spouse is to communicate individual needs. After all, your spouse is not a mind reader and shouldn't be required to guess about your needs.

There is also a biblical servant/leader function for husbands, but a careful balance is required between servanthood and leadership. When things get out of balance, the results are power struggles, unmet needs, and other problems.

A clearly distressed couple came to my office one day. The husband, Ray, said, "What do you do when your wife just won't obey God's Word and do what you tell her?"

"What do you mean?" I asked.

"Well she won't mow the grass when I tell her to," he responded.

I turned to Charlotte, his wife, "Tell me about that."

"I did mow the grass as long as I could." Charlotte went on, "He has me driving the school bus morning and evening. I have two preschoolers to care for. I have to sell Tupperware to buy clothes for the kids, and he insists that dinner be ready promptly at 5:00. Besides, why can't he mow it?"

"Oh, she knows. I work all day. When I come home at night, I am tired."

This man thought he knew what his wife was to do—obey him—but he didn't have a clue about his own responsibilities. By the way, the Bible does not tell wives to *obey* their husbands. It tells children to obey parents, husbands to love their wives, and wives to voluntarily follow their husbands whose primary objective is to meet their needs. I will be happy to send a free copy of this book to anyone who shows me a Bible verse telling wives to obey their husbands.

One of the ways that this power principle gets out of balance is when husbands treat their wives like children or half-wits. Many men today are quite bewildered by the fact that women no longer need them to survive. Today's women are often educated, employed, and self-sufficient, and men who treat their wives the way they saw dear old dad treating dear old mom, are not only unsuccessful as husbands but are also often bitter, longing for the "good old days." They blame women for their own failure to learn how to relate to adult women.

Certain elements in today's society—the women's movement, women moving into careers and out of the homes, and the relative ease of divorce—may all have their drawbacks, but one clear benefit they share is that women no longer need to feel trapped in a relationship where they are treated as children and not permitted to grow and develop as individuals. Precisely because a woman can now leave a relationship that is not satisfying, she is also free to stay, not because she has to but because she wants to. For men or women, staying married because we choose to is far superior to the old "I have no choice" option. Having a choice in the matter greatly increases the need and, therefore, the motivation to relate to each other in a healthy way.

I have been discussing this as though unhealthy relating is a problem open only to men. Of course, this is not so. Men can act like parents or like children, and so can women. I was interviewing a man (or trying to) the other day, who was accompanied by his wife.

DR. FOSTER. Mr. Smith, tell me about why you are here.

MR. SMITH. Well, doctor, I—

MRS. SMITH. Oh, he has been so depressed, doctor. Really he just can't seem to do anything right. Isn't that right, Stanley?

MR. SMITH. Yes, I—

MRS. SMITH. You know the other day he couldn't even figure out how to get the lawn mower started. I had to come out and do it for him. Isn't that so, Stanley?

MR. SMITH. Aw—yes, dear.

117

DR. FOSTER. Mrs. Smith, I wonder if you are aware that every time I ask Stan a question, you answer it, and every time he opens his mouth, you interrupt.

MRS. SMITH. Well, I can see we are not going to get very far with you, Dr. Foster.

DR. FOSTER. Perhaps not, but I wonder if you'd mind if I just talked to Stan for a few minutes alone. Would you mind waiting down the hall in the waiting room?

MRS. SMITH. Sure. He's the one who wanted me in here.

Several problems are immediately evident that need to be corrected if this marriage is to become healthy. Mr. Smith has abdicated his leadership role in the marriage. He must become a responsible, assertive leader. Also, he must learn to express the anger that has built up within him and caused him to become depressed, so depressed that he can no longer function normally. Mrs. Smith must release the reins of power and treat Mr. Smith like a man, not a boy. As you can see, there are problems of tyranny (leading to meet personal needs), abdication (not leading, which is also usually to meet personal needs), and identity (when one person becomes too strong and overpowering in the relationship, the other often appears to cease to exist as a unique, worthwhile adult with an identity of his or her own).

One final question to consider, If your needs are not being met by your spouse, at some point should you meet your own needs? The answer is difficult, but I think my answer would have to be a qualified yes, some needs, sometime. I would hasten to add that you might be wise to look seriously at whether the need in question is genuinely a need or only a want. Also, meeting your own needs does not absolve you of the responsibility to meet your spouse's needs. I would hope that meeting your own needs would be done carefully and prayerfully, not just out of habit. There were times when Christ left the masses to be alone for a while (which met His needs for spiritual nourishment). But I am also aware that Christ ultimately sacrificed His own needs for the sake of His bride, the church.

In the next chapter, we'll look at the three "minor" or less frequent problem areas in marriage counseling and then look at some specific issues and questions.

9

Marriage Counseling Issues

The three minor problem areas that merit attention are finances, relatives, and sex. Any one of these can and does end marriages, and the counselor must include them in his mental checklist of marital issues.

Financial Sense

Being stewards, making mutually discussed decisions, maintaining a low debt level, living within one's means, budgeting, planning, and using common sense are all principles involved here. More and more young couples are getting caught up in the web of easy credit, impulse buying, and spiraling debt, which obviously affects their relationship. Divorce lawyers say that in 80 percent of all divorces, finances are a part of the cause.

This is an area in which Christian workers must become involved in guiding, advising, and discipling young couples. There are some good books on Christian principles for financial management. I suggest that if you are going to help a couple with their finances (and more churches are doing just that), take the time to read one or more of these books. They will give more specific help than I could possibly touch upon in these few statements. I will add just one comment to the debt issue. Everyone I know who does financial counseling insists that the couple cut up their credit cards before any work is done to help them get out of debt.

If you are doing just marriage counseling and not specifically financial counseling, it is still a good idea to find out how the bills are paid. I usually ask, "Who writes the checks?" "Who decides what checks will be written?" "Who carries the checkbook?" "Who gives out money when it is needed?" "Does your wife get enough money for household expenses?" "How is that amount decided upon?" There is real power in the purse strings and all too often, wives are left to handle the money by default because husbands simply don't take any responsibility in this area. When finances are handled properly, both spouses are communicating and listening.

It's All Relative

I have seen marriages end for no apparent reason other than relatives. The principle to remember here is, "Don't let anything or anyone jeopardize your marriage." In general, problems come from being too close or too involved with relatives. Living with them, having them live with you, living next door, working for or with relatives, all put added stress on your marriage. Sure, you love your parents, but that doesn't mean you should lose your marriage as a result.

Someone once said, "Relatives are like fish. After three days they stink." I will freely admit that when I visit my parents, both of whom I love dearly, I live by this three-day rule. Even if I am going to be in the area for a week or so, I arrange some other place to visit after two-and-a-half days. I may be gone for a day or two, then perhaps return for three more days. I don't consider this cruel or heartless. I consider it to be a means of protecting a relationship that is important to me. It also gives my parents a break, which is good for them too.

It is often helpful to guide a couple into prioritizing their relationships. Ask, "What would be your most important relationship, next most important, and so on? If you have a conflict between a level one priority and a level four priority relationship, which one should give in?

Usually, it is not necessary to do a "parentectomy" (removing inflamed parents from the proximity of the adult child before they burst). But when parents will not abide by the rules and guidelines given to them, sterner action is needed. It is important to remember that in general, the older parent needs (emotionally) the adult child and that child's family more than the adult child needs his parents. This being the case, it is not at all unusual for parents to give in and make the adjustment that is required of them.

You can coach your counselee to lovingly confront her parents by saying something like, "I don't like it when you tell me what to do with my children or when you put down my husband. In the future, when I come to visit, I will stay only as long as you can remember this rule. When you violate it, I will leave. I will be back another day, but that day's visit will be over."

Tell your counselee it is absolutely essential for her to follow through with her threat. The counselee will have an opportunity to do so during her very next visit with her parents, because the child's warning will probably not be "heard" or accepted by the parents. She will have to give credibility to her statement by leaving when the rules are violated. I often have to tell couples to move, quit, sell, kick out, or do whatever is necessary to protect their marriages.

Sexual Satisfaction

Sexual relations within marriage are supposed to be enjoyable for both people. Sex is a bond that helps keep the marriage together. When this principle is violated, there is frustration and often guilt. It can affect virtually the entire relationship.

Usually sexual problems are not really sexual problems. Usually they are sexual symptoms of love problems, communication problems, a problem of acceptance, or a problem with being selfish rather than meeting the other person's needs. If you, the counselor, recognize that the sexual symptom is related to one of the four major problem areas, perhaps it is best to tell the couple that you see this as a symptom of another problem and go ahead and treat the real problem rather than the symptom.

Frankly, I am uncomfortable with the idea of Sunday school teachers, church board members, and even pastors and wives doing sex therapy with their parishioners. I believe that sex therapy should be left to those who have been professionally trained to do it. It is not that sex therapy is that difficult. It is not. It is also rewarding. But the techniques are very specific, and you have been trained to know them or you haven't. A lot of misinformation given out by well-meaning people has done a lot of harm.

Having discussed the four primary and three secondary marriage problem areas, we move now to several other questions and issues regarding marriage counseling.

Getting Things Started

Before beginning a marriage counseling session, you should arrange the chairs so that the spouses are almost facing each other, with you sitting facing them.

The couple will initially address you while they are talking, and you will need to constantly encourage them to address their comments to each other. If the chair arrangement forces them to look at each other, it becomes more obvious that they need to communicate with and deal with each other. In conjunction with this, one of the most effective comments a marriage coun-

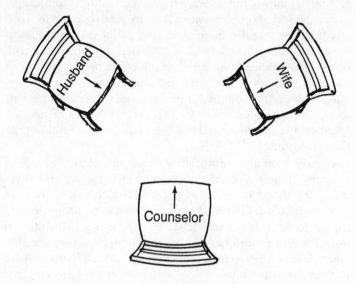

selor can make, when a counselee is complaining about a spouse, is, "There he is, tell him."

When beginning a first counseling session with a couple, I open with a very brief introductory paragraph that sounds something like this:

"I can see you are both here together, so that gives me some idea of what you are here about, but I am going to ask each of you, 'Why are you here and what is happening with you?' It doesn't matter who goes first because I am going to ask the other person exactly the same questions. Who will be first?"

You can get some initial information by watching how the couple handle this decision. It is not unusual for one of them to say, "Let my spouse go first. He (she) is the one who wants to be here." Almost always, someone will volunteer. If they both sit there silently, then you really have your work cut out for you.

In most marriages, one spouse is usually more expressive and communicative while the other spouse is less so. When two unexpressive people are married, it is more difficult to turn that into a healthy relationship.

If they are both quiet, pick one to speak first. It might be good to try to ask the more hostile person to speak first if no one volunteers. That will likely get the counseling session off to a faster start.

When Only One Person Comes for Counseling

Frequently, I get a phone call from someone who says, "My husband and I need marriage counseling, but he won't come. What should I do?"

DR. FOSTER. Did he say he wouldn't come for counseling or do you just *think* he wouldn't come?

CALLER. I have asked him several times if we could go for counseling, and he always says he doesn't need it.

DR. FOSTER. If you made an appointment for next week to come and see me, and if you told your husband you had done that and that you were coming with or without him, but you would like for him to join you, would he let you come?

CALLER. Oh yes, probably. He always says he thinks I am the one who is crazy.

DR. FOSTER. Okay. Why don't you do just that? Make an appointment. Tell him you are coming and he is invited to come if he wants.

Sometimes the husband surprises everybody and shows up at these sessions. When he doesn't, depending on the situation, I'll usually call him after two or three sessions and say, "This is Dr. Foster calling. I think you know your wife has been coming in to see me for some counseling the last few weeks. I usually ask a family member if he would be willing to come in and tell me what he thinks is the problem, so I can get another perspective on this. I am not at home with her during the week to see what is actually going on, so it is often helpful for me to hear somebody else's point of view."

Over 80 percent of the time, the husband will come in at least once after I have used this approach. Most of the time I can get him involved once he has broken the ice and come in and knows that I am really willing to listen to his side of the story too. Sometimes I'll say, "This has been very helpful. It occurs to me that you are really in a better position in many ways to be her counselor than I am. You are with her all week. I am with her for just one hour. You have known her longer than I have. You love her, I don't. Besides, you are cheaper. How would you feel about getting involved with the counseling so that eventually you could take over? Really it belongs more with you than with me because you are her husband."

You notice that these statements are 100 percent true. But they also offer face-saving ways of getting involved without his having to admit that he is not perfect. Most of the time, that admission comes once people are involved with counseling. This is especially true if you, the counselor, can admit you have trouble with a certain emotion or level of communication.

Sometimes, when one spouse has been in alone the first time, and I sense the other spouse is open for counseling, I might suggest that the one I have seen, say, "Dr. Foster said to ask if you wanted to come in once by yourself to give him your side of the story, and after that we might want to go in together." If the husband agrees, I will have usually given the first spouse a tentative appointment, so she can say, "Dr. Foster said he would tentatively hold Tuesday at 3:00 P.M. for you, but you should call if you are coming or if you want a different time."

Giving one spouse an appointment time for the other is dangerous territory. If you have any reason to believe it might be resented, don't do it. When the other spouse simply refuses to get involved, it is still okay to see just one person. Remember that the real growth happens when people stop blaming each other and accept the responsibility for their own attitudes, behaviors, and loving communication. This can be accomplished with just one spouse just as easily as two.

Actually, since you have to share the time and attention if both spouses come in for marriage counseling, you can accomplish some things more rapidly than with just one spouse present. The main point, rather bluntly put, is "He may never change. We can't fix him. But are you being everything you can be?" Once the noncounseling spouse sees an improved attitude in the counseling spouse, it is not unusual for that spouse to decide that counseling is a good idea and then join the session.

The Phases of Marriage Counseling

Every person is unique and so is every couple, but there are some similarities in the phases of marriage counseling.

First Session. Phase One is what I call the "missile-throwing stage." The members of the couple fire missiles at each other and defend themselves from incoming missiles. The main words during this phase are *but he, she,* and *you.* There is little or no *I* present. It sounds something like this.

JOHN. She never welcomes me home.
MARCIA. He is only affectionate when he wants something.
JOHN. She is never affectionate. She is always cold.
DR. FOSTER. Why don't you tell her that?
JOHN. You are so cold you must be part Eskimo.
MARCIA. At least I am not like you. Two years ago last July at our family reunion, you went around kissing everybody in sight. It was humiliating.

JOHN. Last Christmas my parents asked me what was wrong with you and why you never smiled. You seem angry all the time.

In the first session, I let most of this go on without much interruption until the close of the session. Notice that both partners are listing grievances, some of them quite old. When one partner scores a point, the other often changes subjects but keeps attacking. There is a tendency for them to bring in reinforcements by "quoting" other people who supposedly agree with them.

Toward the end of the session, I try to do four things. (1) Briefly summarize what I think might be happening: "It sounds like both of you have a good bit of anger. John feels Marcia is a bit low on the affection scale, and Marcia apparently feels John is too high." (2) Provide hope: "Yet I see you both still have a lot of emotion invested in the relationship and you would like it to be better than what it is now. I have worked with a lot of couples like you, and most of them have really benefited from counseling." (3) Get a commitment to return, i.e. "I am sure you both knew we weren't going to be able to wave a magic wand and fix this overnight. I would like for us to set a time to come back next week and get to work. Okay?" (Get answer from both.) (4) Tell them what to expect: "Every couple is different, but most couples come once a week and see some significant improvement within about six to ten visits."

Unless one member of the couple has invested his or her heart elsewhere or unless the wall has grown so high that it takes extra time to dismantle it, most couples will feel much better about each other within that period of time.

Second Session. The missile-throwing stage is still very much in evidence. I will sometimes give homework in the first session, depending on the situation, but I will almost certainly give an assignment in the second session. Here are the most common assignments I give.

First, "Spend a half-hour a day alone together talking. During this time there can be no music or TV and no criticism of each other. Out of thirty minutes you should be talking half the time and listening half the time. Husband, it will be your responsibility to initiate this, so if it doesn't get done, we will know who is responsible. Don't just demand a time. Find out what is a good time. Negotiate it together."

You can see there are several benefits to this assignment. Having the husband responsible is one benefit. Learning to negotiate the time is another, in addition to the actual time invested trying to get to know each other in a noncombative atmosphere. By the time the couple come for counseling, they have forgotten how to do this. Also, there is a benefit in just trying to complete the assignment. In a way it is almost like the two of them are together for the first time in a long while, trying to accomplish something together, namely, doing the assignment.

Second, I urge some couples to go out on a date once a week. Every couple is not ready for an entire evening together. Some might end up doing each other bodily harm. But when they can do it, they are reminded of what they liked about each other.

The third homework assignment may surprise many readers, but I encourage some couples not to say anything negative to each other until the next session. The reason is that in a constantly hostile environment, it is difficult to feel closeness or warmth. With different couples, I may encourage them to give five to six "I" messages per day. ("I" messages are defined elsewhere in the book.)

In the second session I gradually begin the educational or instructional phase of counseling. Be sure your comments are brief, hardly ever more than a few sentences at a time. I make a special effort to be evenhanded in the initial "giving feedback" times. For instance, I might say that one person is speaking the truth without love and the other love without truth. Or both people are taking too much responsibility for their spouse's behavior and not paying enough attention to their own.

Sessions two through six are spent trying to get the individuals to stop focusing on *but he* and start focusing on *but I*. When they do this, it is the "growth phase" of counseling. No real growth can take place until people will look at themselves. Everything before that is only preparatory. When they do begin to look at themselves, however, the growth that takes place can happen quite rapidly.

Third Session. By the third session I try to spend at least a half-session seeing the individuals alone. This is important because many people have different personalities when they are with their spouses than when they are by themselves. If you see a big difference in the personalities, you will want to note that and try to help remove the obstacles to being themselves within the relationship. Also, if there is another man or woman involved and the other spouse doesn't know it, this will be your first chance to ask the individual privately about it. If you have sensed unusual hesitation in one of the members of the couple in the sessions before this, go ahead and ask if there is someone else involved.

Do this questioning very carefully, almost apologetically. Guarantee confidentiality and do not tell the spouse what you hear. Let the individual know that whatever you discuss privately is going to be kept private. I generally say this at the beginning of the individual session. Sometimes I can get the couple to double up on sessions in the third week, so I can see each partner for an hour.

If one of the individuals does confess to being involved with someone else, ask if there is still involvement. If it is in the past, keep it in the past. Don't make someone confess to a spouse something that is already over. All this will do is make the person feel bad. If the person has not ended it, then it might be appropriate to explain that marriage counseling is almost useless when a third person is still actively involved. If the answer is no, offer to see that person alone for further counseling. Also, if there is no willingness to end the relationship, I encourage the individual to tell this to the spouse. Of course, you may decide to take a different position on this issue and go ahead with the counseling even though a spouse is still involved with a third party. That is certainly up to you. My advice in this book is not the gospel according to Timothy.

Sessions Four through Eight. Generally the couple will spontaneously bring up an incident or argument that didn't go well. Use that incident as a way of teaching and guiding the couple to different ways of expressing, relating, communicating, arguing, decision making, or whatever. Use the example of what didn't go well as an opportunity to teach them the basic principles that they need to learn for successful marriage. I say to the couple, "This is only one incident, but let's over-analyze it a bit. Let's see what we can learn from it." Be sure to encourage them for things that they have done right. When you see them reacting differently from what they did two months ago, point it out. Tell them you like what you see.

It's hard for counselors to realize the power they may have over people. To some couples, the counselor is a surrogate father. To others, a priest, a referee, a teacher, or a coach. I like the teacher/coach model myself, because it acknowledges the importance of encouragement and feedback, but it also places the responsibility for practice and change clearly with the couple.

One role that I don't like is that of a judge. The couple will almost certainly try to put you in that role in the early stages of counseling. They will say things like, "Do you think that was right?" or "Would you sit there and let him do that?" or "Don't you think that was a terrible way to act?" or "What would you do if your wife did that?" I explicitly say to the couple, "I am not wearing a black robe, and I don't want to be your judge. The important thing is not how I feel about it, but how you felt about it."

Sessions Eight through Ten—Termination Phase. When it is time to terminate, both the counselor and the couple usually know it. Rather than stop all of a sudden, when a couple have had two or three very good weeks in a row, I suggest they may come back in two weeks instead of one. Sometimes we find out that the first week went fine, but the second went poorly. Then we go back to weekly visits for a few weeks. In the termination phase, I will generally go to two weeks between sessions for two or three sessions, and then to one month between sessions for a time or two. I always leave the door open. When we are in what we think is the last session, I tell them, "If you run into a problem that you are not able to take care of yourselves within a reasonable period of time, come back in at once and we will work it out rather than let it get out of hand. Otherwise, have a good time, congratulations, and you know where I am."

Separations: The Good, the Bad, and the Ugly

In general, separations are not good for marriages. Most of the time separation means "halfway divorced," and it is very often somebody's way of getting to date and act single without having to wait for a divorce. Worse yet, separation is often somebody's way of trying out the single life and/or one particular girlfriend or boyfriend, without having to break the marriage legally.

Often the spouse who is waiting at home for the errant spouse to make a decision is thinking, *anything is better than divorce.* Sometimes the unfaithful spouse has pangs of guilt and returns home, only to leave again a week or two later. This revolving-door phase can go on for as long as a year or more with as many as a half-dozen episodes of a spouse moving out. In many cases, this phase will go on as long as the waiting spouse is willing to put up with it.

But let's look at this condition for a moment. When the man moves out on his wife and moves in with his girlfriend, he is physically joining (physically "married" to) the girlfriend. Then when he comes back home, he does the same with his wife. And then, with all the moving out and moving back in, the waiting wife has allowed herself to participate in a multiple marriage. Physically, she is one of two wives. I don't think this is right, and frankly, I think she is so desperate to keep him that she is violating herself and her principles. She may have good motives, but I think the behavior is wrong and something is out of balance.

You might want to suggest that the waiting spouse take the errant spouse back once, as long as he/she agrees to come for counseling. However, the errant spouse must understand that by leaving again, the waiting spouse would be put in a position of "sharing" with another person, which the waiting spouse believes is wrong. Therefore, if the spouse leaves again, the marriage will be terminated. So, the suggestion is to forgive once, but establish certain limits and conditions.

I don't have the wisdom to say what is right and wrong for every situation, and I don't want to be a judge. I don't suggest that you as a counselor should tell someone to "move out," "kick out," or "take back." Most of us have a hard enough time handling our own lives without telling other people what to do with theirs. Counseling does not mean acting as a judge or decision maker for other people's lives; it means acting as a guide and coach. We may give messages such as, "If you do this, that will happen" or "Have you considered this idea?" or "Are you aware of such and such?" The decision and the responsibility must remain the counselee's. Many people will ask what the Bible says, but for the most part, they already know. They certainly know that it was not God's will for their spouse to be unfaithful and to break the marriage vow, and they know that God wanted the marriage to be permanent and happy. They are going to have to make their own decisions about what to do next.

In a few rare situations I will recommend a separation. The

first is when there is such hostility between the two that they are destroying what little love and respect they may have left for each other. This is what I call a "working separation." In a working separation, (1) both spouses clearly acknowledge that they are still in an exclusive relationship (no dating); (2) they are involved in ongoing counseling, either as individuals or as a couple (preferably both); and (3) under the guidance of their counselor, they are spending time with each other. These times with each other are gradually increased, as the ability to stay together without fighting is improved. Initially, I may suggest that they meet at a restaurant for coffee, for fifteen to twenty minutes. This may be their only contact in the first week. It may be all that they can handle. They would arrive at the restaurant separately and leave separately. This brief, positive time is gradually increased until both people are ready to handle living together once again.

The second situation that may require separation occurs when a child needs protection against parental abuse. This is particularly true with sexual abuse. It is surprising to me how often a spouse will side with the other spouse and leave a child who reports being sexually abused in the same household in a desperate and difficult as well as destructive situation.

In most states, a counselor of any kind is *required* by law to report suspected cases of child abuse. There is no confidentiality regarding the law in these cases. The child must be protected. By the way, this is the sole exception to the previous statement that we should not let anything endanger the marriage.

Divorce Counseling

People will sometimes ask me, "As a Christian psychologist, do you do divorce counseling?" The answer is definitely yes. What is divorce counseling? It is helping individuals adjust to the crisis of a failed marriage and the resultant blow to their self-confidence. Divorce counseling also tries to find out what the individual may have done wrong in the marriage and help the individual learn how to do things differently. Thus, it is necessary to deal with the guilt feelings that virtually always accompany a divorce.

I believe it is appropriate for Christians to do divorce counseling because there is no reason not to. It is not appropriate for Christians to judge and condemn one another. Divorced persons are in crisis and have already experienced enough rejection without having to endure that of the counselor too. If they cannot turn to the church and receive understanding, love, and acceptance, where should they go for it?

Once in a while a couple in counseling decides to divorce. Usually that is because another man or woman is involved who one spouse is unwilling to give up. The couple will often ask, "What and how do we tell the children?" This is what I tell them: "First of all, your children are not likely to be surprised. They know there has been trouble, and they have friends at school who have been going through the same thing. Second, tell them together. Third, research has shown that there are some clear differences between the children who have problems adjusting and those who don't."

Children who are likely to develop problems are in situations where the parents are continually putting each other down, giving the child the message, "Your mom (or dad) is a bad person." To avoid this problem don't blame or criticize each other. Describe the problem as "ours." Next, children who have problems are those who lose a parent through the divorce. To avoid this, reassure the child that mom will always be mom and dad will always be dad. This is a hard enough time for kids to handle without feeling rejected by their mom or dad. You are divorcing each other, not the children. Reassure the child, "I will always love you."

Finally, children who feel guilt or responsibility for the divorce are the ones who will develop emotional problems. To prevent this, tell them explicitly that the divorce is not their fault and that they had nothing to do with it. You might want to add that if anything, you stayed together as long as you did because of them. Younger children are particularly susceptible to this guilt response. Ask them if they have any questions. They may say, "Is this because I got a D in math?" or "Is this because I fight with my sister?" Reassure them that this is a problem between mom and dad, that it is not a problem between parents and children, and that it is not their fault in any way.

10

Dealing with Grief

What Is Grief?

What is grief? Perhaps this emotion is different for each person, but it usually refers to the emotion of loss and sadness when someone or something in which emotion has been invested has been taken away. I felt it was necessary to include a whole chapter on this subject because as caring Christians, readers of this book will have the opportunity to minister to someone experiencing grief. You can help grieving people through the valleys, or you can make things harder for them. I hope that by being informed, you will find it easier to help.

People who are hurting need your caring and support, not your sermons, lectures, or condemnation. A gentleman by the name of Joe Bailey tells the story of losing his young son through a tragic death. Mr. Bailey says that the visit that meant the most to him was a man who came to the door, sat and listened, cared and, after about an hour, left. Later, Mr. Bailey realized the man had never uttered a word (*The Last Thing We Talked About* by Joseph Bailey).

Compare that story with this one, which is also true. A seminary student and his wife lost their two-year-old daughter through a sudden death. The young mother was understandably grief stricken and quite tearful. Very shortly after the death, a professor from the seminary came over to the house.

He told the young mother, "Now, mother, when you cry, your baby cries in heaven, so let's have none of that."

I met that mother two years later. She was so depressed by that time that she had to be admitted to a psychiatric hospital. Treatment consisted of various methods of helping that mother go back and get in touch with the feelings she had covered up. When she felt the loss, said good-by to her little daughter, and faced and expressed unresolved other feelings, such as her anger at God for taking her daughter and anger at the professor for his stupidity, her depression lifted. Remember, feelings that are bottled up can cause depression. That's what happened in her case.

I would like to give you a different perspective. A somewhat different account comes from two dear friends of mine who, last year, lost their son in a construction accident. The young man had recently married, and he was my oldest daughter's youth pastor. Here is their statement.

"I have always heard that grief was the utmost soul-wrenching torrent of emotional agony. I didn't experience it that way. When I realized how badly my son was hurt (he wasn't declared officially dead until some two days after the accident, but there was no brain activity at all from the moment of the accident) and I realized that he would not recover, I slipped into the rest room and sobbed for five minutes or more. Then I found myself praying that God would revive and restore my son. The tears stopped.

"That night was Wednesday, which was our normal family night. We all eat together every Wednesday and have a time of praying, studying, and sharing. Of course, we met that night, but while it was not all fun and games, neither was it all gloomy. It was quite bearable. There were moments of tears and loss, but also moments of actual lightness and even laughter. I remember (and this may sound strange but it's true) our pastor asked me why we had decided to donate all of his organs. I told him it was because the family didn't want any organ playing at the funeral.

"Later someone played the song our son had sung at church the Sunday before he died. Our family is all musical, and somehow the song brought out the loss, the incredible loss. All the things we had planned, all of our dreams and hopes, he was a part of them, such a central part, and he was gone."

The couple sometimes laughed while they told their story. Sometimes they seemed uplifted and worshipful. Sometimes they cried. From what I have seen of grief, grief is like that. Sometimes it is quiet and peaceful, sometimes overwhelming, and sometimes even a bitter sort of laughter, a mixture of happy, warm memories, which frequently reminds one of the loss and leads to tears.

The tears we shed over the loss of a loved one or a relationship validate the love that existed. If you and I have been friends for five years and tomorrow I am to leave for Alaska, I have to wonder how much my presence really meant to you if you don't shed a tear. Tears and love go together. There is no such thing as love without the risk of pain and loss. You can avoid grief if you never get involved with anybody, but it's not much of an existence. Grief is real, it is necessary, it may be different for different people, but it is definitely linked with love.

The Stages of Grief

You may have read or heard of the different stages of grief. Sometimes people get the idea that these are distinct, discrete, totally separate phases that always occur in the same order, never miss a stage, and never deviate. This is simply not true. Because people are different, they all react differently. One family may have always used laughter as a way of relating, expressing, and getting through tough times while another family may have used another method. Obviously these families are going to have some differences when they grieve.

On the other hand, there are some general similarities in what often does occur. If you know that these similarities occur, you won't be surprised when counselees go through the different stages. It's important to let them go through each phase because that is a part of the process of facing a loss. It takes some preparation to say good-by, and the mind cannot simply do it all at once. This process is neither sick nor ungodly. It is perfectly normal. As a counselor, your job, if there is any job other than simply listening and caring, is gradually interpreting or suggesting the presence of the next feeling that the grieving process would likely produce and that the grieving person might need to recognize.

Denial

You may have noticed some of these stages in the account told to me by my friends who lost a son. "I realized that he would not recover." The reference here was to the end of the first stage of grief, denial. Tell anyone a tragic event, and the response will almost always be "No," "Oh no," or even "Oh, God, no." These are statements of denial. Even though this couple's son showed a consistently flat brain wave (no activity at all), it took a while for the parents to realize what that meant. This is not unusual. It is normal. Initially, we simply cannot believe that we are being faced with such a death or loss. We are not emotionally prepared for death or significant loss. It is probably good that we are not. If we expected sudden death of loved ones at any moment, we would have a hard time relating closely to them and investing our emotions in them.

You may notice that I used the phrase "death or significant loss." This is because grief is broader than just death. I have a close friend with whom I sang duets. I moved to another state, leaving that friend. It was months before I could listen to the tapes of us singing together. I was feeling grief over the loss of regular contact with a friend. Of course, I have experienced that feeling with other people when I moved too.

It seems so thoughtless to me when people say, "Don't cry. He's in heaven." It's thoughtless because the reason I am grieving is precisely because the loved one is in heaven. I have lost contact with him. If that's true, then I can lose contact with people without their going to heaven and still feel grief.

When someone is in the denial phase, you might say something like, "What a loss" or even "It's hard to face it, isn't it?"

People can feel grief over the loss of their legs, eyesight, a job, the ability to play baseball, health, stability, financial security, self-respect, and many other things. Some time ago I knew of a husband and wife who found out that the husband had multiple sclerosis. They had known for a year that he had the symptoms and that multiple sclerosis was the most likely diagnosis. But they had been able to deny that to themselves until a certain conclusive test came back from the lab. Don't misunderstand. I don't blame them for denying it until they couldn't deny it anymore. As I say, that's normal. When they were finally faced with the results of that test, they faced the reality and their step one, denial, was over.

Typically after this, grieving persons who are not denying any longer feel some of the pain of the loss on a conscious level. So, because they are not yet prepared to face the whole thing, they move out of that intensity of feeling to another stage of grief. While some may move back into denial, and some may move into another stage, most people move into the bargaining stage.

Bargaining

This bargaining stage was also evident in my friend's account of his grief. He said that the feeling of loss was overwhelming, and he began to pray that his son would be healed. He was bargaining with God. It was a way of saying, "Okay, I can't deny the reality of his condition anymore, but I can try to change the reality."

It is easy to see these stages by watching your child when his mother calls him to come inside and wash up for dinner. First, the child denies that he hears her calling. After it is so obvious that he can no longer hold to that excuse, he says, "But can't I stay five minutes longer? Just a little while longer?" He is bargaining as a way of coping with the loss of playtime. Again, there is nothing wrong with trying to strike a bargain. If a loved one was dying, I think I would want to do anything, including bargaining, to keep from losing that person.

When someone is in the bargaining stage you might say something like, "It's easier to face the loss when you feel like you are trying to do something to help, isn't it?" Or if you want to suggest a feeling on the next level, you might say, "That's irritating, isn't it?" or "I can see why you might be angry." By suggesting the next feeling or the next stage, you are helping the person go through the process of grief.

Anger

The next stage many people go through when they see that the bargaining stage isn't working is anger. You can just hear a grieving father say, "We'll bring in the specialists! The best money can buy!" (bargaining). And you can hear the physician say, "I am sorry. That's not going to do you any good. Your daughter is dead." That produces a torrent of rage from the parent, "Well, aren't you going to try to revive her? All you guys are interested in is making money. Why won't you even try?" You can see that the failed bargain often leads a person into anger.

It is understandable that someone who was in the process of bargaining with God for healing, only to be faced once again with the harsh reality of loss, could become angry with God. "Why do I bother to ask You for anything? When I really need

You, where are You?" Many (but not all) grieving people feel some of these feelings. Again, looking at the example of the child playing, you can see as he gives up on the bargaining because mom says "right now," the child throws down his toy and says angrily, "Boy!" or "It's not fair!"

If someone is in the anger stage, you might say, "It almost feels better to blame someone, doesn't it?" Or perhaps, "It's easier to face the loss when you can focus all your emotion and anger on just one person, isn't it?" Or you might suggest, "The anger feels better than the grief, doesn't it?"

Depression

The next stage of grief is often depression. It is sadness, but not the sadness of facing the loss. It is more like the sadness that comes from the flatness, the discouraged feeling that comes from shutting down emotions. It is as if the grieving person knows that the loss is coming, and the only thing he can finally think of to do to keep from facing that loss is to shut down his whole emotional system.

I have seen people stay in this stage for years, but usually it doesn't last nearly that long. Because the person is already feeling discouraged, it is easy for the counselor to suggest that the feeling underneath the depression is a feeling of loss. The suggestion might sound like this, "It's really hard to just feel that loss right now, isn't it? It's almost like it would be easier to shut off all of your feelings."

Acceptance

The final stage is acceptance of the death or significant loss. This will require some times of sadness. Don't try to change this; it is appropriate for someone to be sad after experiencing a loss. But as I have indicated before, the person is usually not sad and overwhelmed twenty-four hours a day. Many different moods and emotions may come and go.

For a person in the last stage, the sad times still come, but they last for shorter periods of time, and they become less intense. Gradually the time between the sadness gets longer and longer. From time to time something will trigger that sad or grief feeling. The person needs to feel that when it happens and then go on. The feeling is painful, but it doesn't last.

The Necessary Word, Good-By

Maybe you don't believe in magic words, but in the area of handling grief, there is one word with almost magical properties, the word *good-by*. People will often call me and say, "We've had a death in the family. What can we do to make sure we are handling the emotions correctly? I want to prevent emotional problems from developing."

I tell them all much the same thing, "Go up to the body (open or closed coffin) and say a few sentences (out loud) to the lost loved one, ending with the word *good-by*. Just tell him what he meant to you and that you'll miss him."

Someone just got upset with me again. I can hear you yelling, "But that person is not there in that body. He is in heaven." I know that. The deceased is in heaven. That person may very well not hear a word. So what's the point of saying anything? The point is that the living need to say something to help them adjust to the loss. The one in heaven doesn't need to hear it, but the living need to say it.

If the last word is *good-by*, that will be like a period at the end of a sentence. It's a little thing really, but it indicates that the entire sentence is over. *Good-by* is the period at the end of the earthly relationship with that person. And, while I don't know why, I do know that it makes a big difference if it is said out loud rather than merely thought. There is a difference between thinking and sending a natural message. Saying it out loud so that it can be heard makes it more real.

I referred to children a moment ago. I am often asked if children should go to funerals. My answer is, if the child had a relationship with the person, then yes, the child should go and say good-by like everybody else.

Handling Divorce

Persons experiencing another kind of grief go through many of the same steps. Many readers will have the opportunity to work with people in this situation. I refer primarily to persons who are being divorced against their will. They would rather reconcile, but the spouse is not willing. These individuals are losing a loved one, a home, a form of security, a means of social acceptance, freedom from the hassles of dating, and much more. In many ways, divorce is harder to handle than death. There is no stigma or sense of being a failure in being widowed, but the divorced person must deal with this plus rejection. In a divorce, an individual is being consciously and deliberately rejected by the person he has been closest to, the person who knows him best, the one he gave the most to, the one to whom he was the most vulnerable. It cannot be easy for an individual to handle all these feelings.

The person going through this experience needs your caring, understanding, and acceptance, which are appropriate and godly responses. As someone who has accepted the challenge of representing the Wonderful Counselor by counseling the bereaved and hurting, you need to love the divorcing person. Judging, condemning, and preaching are all inappropriate.

Counseling with the bereaved requires listening and caring more than anything else. Lectures or other attempts to get a counselee to stop hurting before it is appropriate are not in his best interest. Even though grief has typical stages, everyone is different and will react uniquely. Grief occurs with losses other than death. Grief might also occur at the loss of a love, a job, a house, a marriage.

11

Counseling Spiritual Problems

As I sit down to write this chapter, I realize that what I have outlined here is a whole book, not just a chapter. In addition, the exact determination of what is and isn't a spiritual problem may very well differ in some regard depending on theological interpretations. The treatment may vary for the same reason. Nevertheless, some general problems occur quite often. I will try to cover those that are defined as problems by the counselees, that is, people saying, "I have a problem." Therefore we can avoid the issue of whether or not the counselor thinks it's a problem.

Bad Example

Before we get into what to do, let's look at an example of what *not* to do.

KATHY. I have been feeling so out of it lately. It's like I just don't seem to care about anything. I am just going through the motions.

PASTOR. I notice you missed church last week.

KATHY. I just couldn't get motivated.

PASTOR. You know the Bible says to forsake not the assembling of yourself together.

KATHY. I know, but I—

PASTOR. Well, I don't see how you can expect to feel right if you let your spiritual life go.

KATHY. It's just that I have been feeling kind of distant.

PASTOR. What you need to do is repent of your sins and get right with God.

What's wrong with this counseling? The counselor is too busy judging, condemning, and telling. There is no listening. This can be a problem with any kind of counseling, but it is a particular temptation with spiritual counseling. I think that is because spiritual counseling includes values much more than other counseling. Most people can grasp the idea that counseling for emotional problems is to be nonjudgmental and a counselor is not to force his set of values on the counselee. But even when a counselor understands that, it is a different matter when spiritual ideas are involved, because spiritual issues have inherent values. If the counselor is ever going to be critical and judgmental, it will be in the spiritual area. If the counselor is ever going to try to force his values on someone, it will be in spiritual counseling.

Most Typical Spiritual Problems

I do not intend for this portion of the chapter to be interpreted as a statement of the things that most Christians need to work on or as a statement of the spiritual problems that most commonly exist in the twentieth-century Christian church. Rather, it is a listing of the spiritual problems most often brought by people to counselors. (Problems people have but don't know about will be discussed in the next section.)

"I'm angry at God. Bad things happen." When they do, it's not fun. That's why they are called "bad" things. We live in a scientific cause-and-effect culture. It is not unusual or ungodly for someone to ask, "Why did this happen?"

Have you ever agreed to do some service or ministry, only to find that you got criticized for it, even attacked? Or perhaps you have worked many hours on a Sunday school lesson, a solo, or a presentation for church, only to find that your car won't start or you can't find your keys. It's annoying.

People who really do believe that God is involved in their lives, and has power over this world, are the very same people who are perhaps the most susceptible to feeling as though their Master is being too harsh, never letting up. The piling up of trouble upon trouble, disappointment upon disappointment, begins to feel overwhelming, too heavy to carry. They become angry at the One they think is doing the piling. They become angry at God instead of being thankful in all things. They sarcastically snap at God, "Thanks a lot!"

What can you do as someone endeavoring to represent the Wonderful Counselor? What can you do to help people who are feeling powerless, picked on, and put out? The principles for this kind of counseling are virtually identical to general counseling. The first thing you need to do is communicate understanding, say things like, "That sounds awful," "What a day," "Boy, that is annoying," "That's hard to understand, isn't it?" "It starts to feel like you are being picked on after a while, doesn't it?" "It doesn't sound fair."

Second, communicate caring. Let them know that it matters to you that they have been having a hard time. Say things like, "I am sorry," "I wish I could have been there," "Oh, that upsets me to hear about you having such a hard time."

Third, guide them toward expressing that anger directly to God. I do it this way. After I have let them talk, and after I have communicated the understanding and caring, I simply say, "I was wondering if you have told God about your feeling angry with Him?" The Bible is full of examples of people communicating honestly and directly to God and, by so doing, being able to release all their feelings. Psalm 13 begins with just such an expression.

How long, O LORD?
Will You forget me forever?
How long will You hide Your face from me?
How long shall I take counsel in my soul,
Having sorrow in my heart daily?
How long will my enemy be exalted over me?

By delivering his feelings directly where they belonged, David was able to move from that position to one in which he was more aware of God's goodness and man's need to trust. By the end of the psalm, David said, "But I have trusted in Your mercy; / My heart shall rejoice in Your salvation. / I will sing to the LORD, / Because He has dealt bountifully with me."

In addition to getting the angry person to talk to God, you also may want to help him reaffirm his faith as David did, by asking, "What do you really believe about God's care and His plan for you?" Once the person's mind has been freed from the anger by expressing it, and once he reexamines what he believes about God's love and trustworthiness, you have nothing left to do. You have helped point someone to God with just a few words and no sermons or condemnation.

"Life is hard. Doing what God wants is painful." Life is often hard. Regarding ourselves dead to sin often means saying no to very natural desires or pleasures. Often, to do God's will, we need to look at the long-range consequences of a behavior rather than the short-range ones. Most Christians know this, but let's not forget that it does imply that the thing we are saying no to is more enjoyable in the short run. It's okay to feel badly for a moment about the loss of something pleasurable.

I would hope, however, that we would be able to focus on God and His plans, rather than on the lost desired object or experience. To stare at the sinful desire and not at the Master will get us into trouble. But the way to help the person who is experiencing this is not with sermons or even Bible verses. We are to communicate understanding and caring and gently guide counselees. Let's look at an example.

BOB. Well, I stayed away from Carol all week like we talked about last time. I never called her once. But this is really rough.

TOM. It's hard to stay away from someone you care about.

BOB. That's for sure. If God wasn't so clear about not marrying non-Christians, I'd never even try to break off with Carol.

TOM. I know it hurts. I'm sorry.

BOB. Me too. I guess I really do believe that God knows what He is doing. But it sure is not the way I'd do business.

TOM. It's hard to understand how something that hurts is supposed to be good for you, isn't it.

BOB. That's the truth. It doesn't seem fair. Carol is the best thing that ever happened to me.

TOM. Oh?

BOB. Well, I guess humanly I think so. Spiritually, I guess not.

TOM. I notice there is a difference.

BOB. Yeah.

TOM. I wonder how you feel about that.

BOB. Not good.

TOM. I hear a battle going on.

BOB. That's for sure.

TOM. Which side do you want to win?

BOB. I don't know.

TOM. Bob, you are going to feed one side or the other, and that is the side that will grow and win.

BOB. I guess if I want the Spirit to win, I have to really work on feeding my spirit this week, huh?

TOM. I guess so.

Notice the confrontation here when Bob said his girlfriend

was the best thing that ever happened to him. The counselor could have launched into a little (or big) sermon about how God was really the best thing that had ever happened to him, but a raised eyebrow, a little doubt in the voice of the counselor, and the single response "Oh?" can lead Bob into confronting his own statement. This is far more effective than the counselor's confronting it.

"God wants one thing. I want another." A spiritual conflict exists when a person knows what God says, but he is going to do something his way anyway. The person (unlike the one in the previous example who is struggling to obey) is in a state of rebellion. What do you do to help?

Certainly, most people in this state are aware that they are going their own way. Nevertheless, a few may have deluded themselves and have conveniently "forgotten" what God wants. So, remind them, but don't overdo it. Tell them once. Briefly state your reasons. Here's an example.

CARL. You have been in this church a long time, Dick. You know what the Bible says about adultery. It says it's wrong. It's a path that leads to destruction. I am concerned. How do you deal with this going against what you have always believed and taught?

DICK. I deal with it by saying I've changed my mind. I'm doing what I want to, and I don't need sermons from you.

CARL. I understand that. It just doesn't seem like you.

DICK. I don't want to talk about it. I'm doing what I want. I have spent all my life doing what other people wanted, and there never seems to be a time when it's my turn. I'm tired of waiting. I'm making it my turn now.

CARL. Obviously I can't stop you. All I can do is warn you that what you are doing is dangerous, painful in the long run, and not worth it.

DICK. Warning noted.

CARL. It's making me very sad. It's like watching a friend take poison. I want you to know I will be available anytime to talk, help, or whatever.

"I want to know God (better)." Sometimes you have the joy of sharing with people who are spiritually open and receptive. How do you feed people who are hungry? You don't talk about food, you take them to the bread. You don't have to give complicated answers to hungry people. You just show them the bread. God's Word is spiritual food. The spirit will grow if it is fed and shrink if it is starved.

How do you get to know people better? Spend time with them, listen to them, think about them, study them. It is the same with God. People who want to know God can do so. You can augment Bible reading, prayer, meditation, and worship with Christian books about God and, in the background, good Christian music. But the basic building blocks are heavy Bible study and a heart that wants to know God and be His more than anything else.

"My spiritual life is flat, dull, and uninspired." Breathes there a Christian who has never experienced this? Here again, preaching and condemning are not the answers. For someone who is feeling flat spiritually, the odds are high that he is not controlling his input; therefore, his spiritual output is out of control.

I remember a Christian young man telling me he was having a problem with impure thoughts. As we looked at how he spent his day and what he put into his mind, we realized that his new job required him to spend three to four hours daily driving his car. That whole time he was listening to music, the main message of which was variations on the theme of "Hey, baby! Let's get it on." Let that be your input for four hours a day, and it doesn't take a Ph.D. to predict that your mental output is going to be the very same, "Hey, baby!"

We agreed that, by way of experiment, he would listen to only Christian music for two weeks, and then we would test his mental output. The Christian music was contemporary, but the words and the message were godly. The result? Godly thoughts and desires. It is appropriate to suggest that people spend more time with spiritual input if they want to have Christian lives that are more vibrant.

Another way to make a Christian life come alive is to do something with it. Suggest that the counselee start witnessing, sharing, visiting, even doing servant behaviors for others.

"What does God want? What is God's will." We live in an age of incredible change. Friends, neighbors, family, and even we are likely to consider major moves and major changes in our lives in the next few years. Schooling, housing, career, marriage, divorce, church membership, the list goes on. And most people who make changes thought and talked about those changes before making them. In other words, they got counsel of some kind, if only informally. What can you do to help?

First, you have to do some thinking and studying on the topic of what God wants from His children, or God's will. If you study this in the Bible, you will find that God is far more concerned with who you are than where you are. God cares far more about your attitude than your address. God wants you to seek Him, trust Him, depend on Him, and serve Him.

I think if you could interview Christ on the subject, He might say that if you've taken care of basic spiritual issues, you can live anywhere you want. Really? Yes, really. Remember, of course, if your mind and heart are focused on God, on being His child and His servant, and if you love Him more than anything, what He wants will be what you want.

I do believe that God, the greatest planner and greatest general of all time, can not only devise a perfect plan for our lives but can also communicate it. Can you imagine even an adequate army major, on the battlefield, not making clear to his troops what he wanted them to do? How much more would a general be clear in his direction? How much more God?

Here are some helpful basic guidelines to use to stay within God's will. First, you must be committed to following wherever God leads. Asking to know God's will so you can decide whether or not you are going to do it will not work. Second, read the Bible and pray, asking for direction. Third, make some move in the direction you are considering to see what happens. Do doors open? Do you feel peace? Do you feel closer to God as you move in that direction? Many people wait for doors to open before they move, but God's doors often operate like the automatic doors at the supermarket. If you just stand back and watch, nothing happens. You have to move toward the door before it opens.

Fourth, it is good to consider your insides. Do you feel a burden for a particular ministry? Do you have the gifts for that ministry? Do other believers you know and respect agree that this sounds like a ministry or direction that fits you?

Fifth, look at your priorities. Write them down. Think and pray about them. If you are married, talk with your spouse about your joint priorities. If your priorities are clear, your decisions will make themselves.

As always, don't tell people what to do when you counsel them. Guide them to look up the important issues. Ask questions. Help them decide, but don't decide for them and then spend your counseling time trying to convince them to do what you have decided. God can lead them directly. He is not obligated to tell you His plan for someone else.

I remember a young man who went to the same Christian college I did. He had accepted the Lord in his senior year of high school, and an elderly woman at the church he was beginning to attend went up to him and said, "God told me you should go to Nyack Missionary College." Not knowing any better, he went. He did poorly because he didn't really belong there, and he went home the first year.

Using Scripture in Counseling

For some, if you are not quoting two Bible verses per sentence, they don't think you are spiritual. Others figure you both already know what the Bible says, and although you may refer to a verse now and then, they would rather talk about their problem and have you listen rather than talk or preach. Of course, one of the problems with too much Bible quoting is that it very easily can sound like preaching.

A notable exception is when people don't know what the Bible says. Then I would say they need to know whether or not they are interested in knowing or willing to find out. Even when it is appropriate to include Bible verses, ideally you should point out those verses, the counselee should read them, and you should guide the counselee into discovering what they mean.

A hurting person is not particularly interested in theological explanations, and a counselee will totally miss the point if you give a long involved response. In counseling, briefer is better. You can actually watch a counselee's eyes glaze over after your second sentence. I rarely say more than two sentences in a row in counseling, because that's all most people in counseling will listen to at one time. There is simply no room within two or three sentences for technical data, like explaining that a passage of Scripture may have been written to combat the influence of a first-century philosophy called "Gnosticism."

When you quote Scripture in counseling, it is unnecessary in most cases to specify chapter and verse to believers because they already are familiar with most passages. The purpose in quoting Bible verses to believers is usually only to remind them of the passage, not to educate them that it exists. On the other hand, nonbelievers don't know what in the world "the second chapter of the second epistle of the apostle Paul to the church in Corinth, verse number 9" means. You are better off just saying, "You know the Bible says—" If they want to know where it says

155

that, you can show them. It's also okay to give a general reference like, "It says in the last chapter of John—"

Some counselees may be hostile or resistant to religious ideas or Bible quoting in general. For those people, you might refer to the truth of Scriptures in a general way. You might say, "There is a saying, 'Speak the truth in love.' I think that might be a guideline for us."

Another problem with heavy dependence on Bible study in counseling is that it makes the mistaken assumption that counseling is searching for "the answer." Counseling is rarely that. As I have said before, counseling is mostly support, understanding, and general guidance. Your telling someone else "the answer" to a problem is not counseling. If you are convinced that you are called to give people answers all day long, I suggest you get a job at an information desk somewhere, but don't counsel.

I know I will be misquoted and prayed over for that last sentence, but I think I have made it clear that even if there is one clear answer to a problem, reading it to someone is practically useless. Counselors need to guide people into discovering answers for themselves if they are going to act on those answers.

At a convention of the Christian Association for Psychological Studies (CAPS) several years ago, a friend and associate of mine, John Hower, Ph.D., gave a paper on the use of Scriptures in counseling. He has given me permission to use some of his ideas here.

Misuse of Scripture

Scripture has been misused when a counselee feels alienated from the counselor as a result of the way the Scriptures were used. This might happen if the counselor always responded to feelings with a Bible verse. This is especially true if the Bible verse tends to counter or rebuff the feelings expressed. Here is one example of a nonunderstanding rebuff with the use of Scripture.

Bill says, "I just can't change my temper. I have tried. Donna will have to take me the way I am."

The counselor responds, "Ephesians 4:1–3 says the fruit of the Spirit is self-control. God expects you to control yourself. Why should Donna accept you the way you are? God doesn't."

This approach seems to alienate more people than it helps. My response to Bill's "I won't change" might be, "Bill, I am not sure if that's what you really believe or what you would like to believe. It does conveniently let you off the hook. Donna has to do all the adapting, and you get to go on the way you are." Later on, I might ask, "What do you believe about self-control?" Or if appropriate, "What does the Bible teach about self-control?" I try to get him to bring the biblical truth out.

A second related misuse of Scripture would be using Scripture in such a way that the counselee may feel condemned. Christ's purpose was not to condemn the world but to save the world (John 3:17). Many times in Scripture we are warned not to judge others (see Matt. 7:1–2; Rom. 14). This is not to say that confrontation is never appropriate. Second Timothy 3:16 does speak of reproof and correction. There is often a sensitive line between confrontation and judgment, but there is some evidence that effective counselors are able to distinguish between loving confrontation and judgment.

A third inappropriate use of Scripture could be classified as intellectual diversion. This might take the form of argument or intellectualized discussion of a biblical concept. For the counselee-focused counseling I have been advocating, argument becomes a diversion from such things as self-exploration and tends to lead to a purely intellectual interaction. Discussion of a topic such as forgiveness might be interesting to both the counselee and the counselor. However, it often leads the counselee away from his own inner processes.

A fourth inappropriate use of Scripture would be using passages of Scripture as defenses against feeling certain emotions. For example, a person dealing with a loss might be presented with a verse of hope and victory before he had really experienced the reality of despair. He might be encouraged to have a false sense of victory and block from his awareness some of the normal feelings related to the separation and grieving processes.

Appropriate Use of Scripture

Appropriate uses of Scriptures should be expressions of understanding and caring. The counselor's responses should convey the message that God understands the difficulty. The Scriptures should be relevant to the current therapeutic issue. It might be tempting to pull out a passage of Scripture that is only tangentially related to the issue, but the passage should reflect the same empathy as other interventions that have been shown to lead the counselee toward openness. A brief comment, which appropriately brings Scripture into a situation that the counselee has presented, shows that the counselor has understood his emotions. Also the counselee could get an inkling that God and the Scriptures are relevant to his distress. For a person struggling with the tension between his ideals and the temptations of his business situation, the counselor might appropriately comment that perhaps this is what Jesus was referring to when he talked about being in the world but not of the world (see John 17:11-16).

A major use of Scripture that would be productive in the counseling process is the presentation of the human drama of biblical characters as models. Many times biblical characters have had to cope with the same issues that are brought up by counselees. For example, the person dealing with feelings of competition and comparison with others could be shown that the disciples had to deal with this tendency (see John 21:20–24). In the psalms David's struggle with his guilt is graphic in terms of the process involved; he initially hid his sin, then agonizingly confessed, and then felt the release of forgiveness. This might be helpful to those who struggle with guilt.

Another appropriate use of Scripture would be to exemplify the growth process. For example, the verse, "He who has begun a good work in you will complete it until the day of Jesus Christ" (Phil. 1:6), gives an indication of the overall process of growth and development that God intends for believers.

Still another use of Scripture might be classified as teaching. For many counselees who largely lack information, this might be very helpful. Some new Christians may need to know the basic codes of conduct that are sanctioned by the Scriptures. For some who lean heavily on the Scripture as authority, a careful look at Scripture might be helpful in clarifying distortions or rationalizations. The counselor should be cautious so that these uses of Scripture do not become the intellectual diversions or condemnations that were mentioned previously.

A counselor might use the Bible to teach someone who is having trouble being an independent, confident individual with personal opinions. Such people often come in with complaints about what others will not let them do or how they are trapped in relationships or how they fear hurting others. They may also complain of how unsatisfactorily their parents did things. The counselor might comment that it is interesting that Jesus was not much interested in pleasing others. He might relate the story in which Jesus' parents questioned Him about what He was doing in the synagogue. Jesus said, "I must be about my Father's business" (Luke 2:49). The point of this story would be that even at age twelve, Jesus seemed to be aware that He had some things to do with His life that might be different from what His parents chose for Him. Jesus expressed similar attitudes in Matthew 12 when He was told that His mother and

159

brother were there, implying that He should drop what He was doing. His reply indicated that He was not bound or limited to His nuclear family, "Whoever does the will of My Father in heaven is My brother and sister and mother" (Matt. 12:50). Jesus displayed a healthy separation from His family relationships. It is evident that this wasn't a rejection, because on the cross He made provision for His mother by telling John, "Behold your mother!" and by telling her, "Behold your son!" (John 19:26–27).

There are numerous other examples of assertiveness. Paul, David, Stephen, and many early unnamed Christians were bold even under persecution. Instructive passages communicate that God has not given us "a spirit of fear, but of power and of love and of a sound mind" (2 Tim. 1:7). These provide models of independence and convey the idea that it is okay to be one's self. This may be sufficient for some; others may know they need to be independent and desire to do so but find themselves unable to achieve it. Many people in this situation are responding to various fears of rejection or some adverse reaction from others and need to explore their fears with the counselor.

Another large group of people experience distress because of blocked emotions. An example would be a female counselee who worries about various problems with her family and children yet feels that she would be complaining if she talked with her husband about her concerns. This person needs encouragement to be able to express her feelings.

A counselor should not, however, be so naive as to think that merely by showing that Jesus had and expressed His emotions, the counselee will suddenly open up and spill his insides. This will not happen. The biblical input is merely part of the whole gradual process of growth and development that takes place in counseling. Bible verses should not be confused with magic words so that the counselor need only wave one over the head of the counselee to produce an instant cure. That is not the case.

Counseling Spiritual Problems
When Someone Has Failed

When Christian brothers and sisters fall, whether it be sexual sin, some incredibly unthinking act, or the result of taking matters into their own hands only to fall face down on the turf, and when they have admitted, faced, or confessed that act, they often need the help of a godly counselor.

These dear folks are hurting, often fearing public knowledge of their behavior and the possible embarrassment and pain to their family, church, and God. They may believe that God forgives them, but they are having a hard time forgiving themselves, facing themselves, and believing that they could do such a thing. Times of such personal crises often require a significant restructuring of self-esteem as in "I am not as hot as I thought I was." If you become aware of a brother or sister who has just been faced with a sinful, imperfect nature, you will do a great service if you will stick your neck out and love that person.

People who have just failed often forget that things Satan intends for evil, God allows for good. Of course, the best example of this is Christ's crucifixion, which Satan brought about hoping to kill off the Messiah, but God allowed to purchase redemption for sinners.

Many of us believe in grace. But that belief is often only "head knowledge." In our hearts we often are very performance oriented. We think we are only loved and accepted for what we can do, for what we can achieve. I know I have had a struggle with this. The idea that people fail is something we can accept, but the idea that we ourselves can fail is awful for us to have to acknowledge. But our friends and family or our church finding out that we have failed is even a more horrible thought. Or, facing them, once they know, may seem to be just too much to handle.

If you find someone in this state, remember that God Himself may have put you in a pivotal position in the life of this person for whom God has definite plans. I am surprised at how often, before all the trouble appeared, the person involved had sincerely asked God to make a change in his life and to bring about significant spiritual growth.

Often, if not always, God brings a low before He can break new spiritual ground with us. Deeper life studies will show us that we have to die to self in order to experience total sellout to God. That makes sense, but few of us realize the pain involved in dying to self. Letting go of what people think of us, dying to the slavery of reputation and public opinion, willing to appear to be a fool, willing to be anything but separate from God, these are requisites of dying to self. After the death comes the new life.

Remember this when you are counseling with someone who has just faced his own worthlessness. God can use that person mightily in that state, but He could hardly use the self-sufficient workaholic at all. I know that God didn't want the person to sin, but He did know about the failing ahead of time. He is quite ready to use this bad time as a time for death, burial, and resurrection to new life in Christ. Guide the person into this truth and God will bless you.

Judging and condemning are to be avoided. If God can hate the sin while still loving the sinner, the counselors must look to the same objective.

God's timing is not our timing, and we can't make people's decisions for them. We must guide people to a point where they can make their own decisions. Trying to force decisions, especially in the spiritual area, is definitely counterproductive.

12

Counseling Family Problems

Family counseling has become a specialty field among professional counselors. I am well aware that this one chapter cannot begin to equip you to go out and compete on a professional level with these trained specialists, but I am also aware that most family problems never make it to a professional family counselor. Most family problems are dealt with informally or not dealt with at all. There are, therefore, some basic principles that can be helpful when you have the opportunity to minister to someone with family problems.

The Problem of Control

Most family problems can probably be summed up in one word, *control*. People don't control at all, they control too much, they don't know how to control, they are being controlled and don't like it, they refuse to be controlled, the wrong things are being controlled, or they don't know how or when to stop controlling.

Think of these problems and the general concept of control when you counsel people with family problems, and more often than not, you will have some idea of what is causing the family stress. Sometimes, especially when more than one family member is present, many different complaints and accusations on many different topics will be aired. This can be confusing, but trying to handle each specific area of conflict may not be as useful as trying to fix the underlying problem of the control conflict.

It is probably a good idea for you to gradually try to direct the counselee's attention to the issue of control. Often you can begin by helping the counselee examine what he believes about control. If he believes something that is reasonable, biblical, and accurate about control, then you, the counselor, need only point out that the method or technique of controlling is not consistent with the belief. You might offer suggestions for him to try that would be more consistent with what he believes. Use the fact that it is "his" belief that things should be a certain way (if the belief is reasonable). This will help the counselee with the motivation to change behavior. He will change to conform more closely to his own beliefs.

If his belief about control seems off base to you, you might try to guide the counselee into challenging his beliefs or perhaps you might use the "pragmatic" approach, which is to point out that his approach isn't working and maybe he ought to try a different one. You can then suggest an approach that you have seen work many times. Here are two examples.

EDITH. I just can't believe Rick. He is twenty-three years old, lies around the house, tells me how to do things, only has a part-time job, and spends most of his money on his dumb model train hobby. Frankly, I feel like I have put in my mothering time and I wish he'd get married or something. He seems to be married to his model trains.

VICKIE. That sounds annoying.

EDITH. Oh, he's a good boy. At least he's not out running around or on drugs or something.

VICKIE. But you believe parenting is supposed to be a temporary job and you feel you have already given Rick a good start.

EDITH. Absolutely.

VICKIE. I assume you have thought of the obvious solution. What are your thoughts on that?

EDITH. What obvious solution?

VICKIE. I just mean asking him to move out or get a place of his own.

EDITH. Oh, I couldn't do that. He couldn't afford it, and I would feel like a louse.

VICKIE. Whatever happened to your belief that parenting is temporary?

EDITH. Well, I do believe that, but I just can't kick him out.

VICKIE. Okay, let's back up. If parenting is temporary, then the primary objective of parenting is to produce a self-sufficient or independent adult, right?

EDITH. I guess so.

VICKIE. Have you accomplished that goal yet? Have you produced an independent adult?

EDITH. I guess not. But I think he is capable.

VICKIE. Exactly. He is capable. I agree. Then maybe the only thing keeping you from becoming a successful parent and him from becoming an independent adult is that he hasn't had to.

EDITH. That's probably true.

VICKIE. A lot of people don't make the final jump until they have to because it's just easier to let someone else take care of them. Edith, it sounds like it's not only going to be better for both of you if he finishes growing up, but you've started to get on each other's nerves. In other words, by not doing it, you are actually damaging the relationship. I know it would be difficult to say, "You've got sixty days," but I know you've done difficult things before as a mother, when they were for the good of your own child.

EDITH. You may be right.

There are several things to observe in this example. First, Edith's beliefs were healthy. It was her behavior that was a little slow. Second, the counselor was the one who actually suggested what Edith's beliefs were. It is apparent that these two women know each other, so it's not unreasonable that Vickie would guess. Also, as I have indicated, if the counselor can get the counselee to agree to a healthy sort of belief about parenting, the counselee is more easily motivated to change. Often the counselor's job is to actually put words to someone's beliefs or philosophies, which is often helpful so that a counselee can examine his own philosophy. It is amazing how often people do things as important as parenting without stopping to really examine what they believe about it. Often, people spend their whole lives following little one-sentence philosophies that they never stop to examine and that may not hold up at all under examination, such as "Never hurt anyone," "Never ask for help," or "It's bad to talk about negative feelings." All these statements greatly affect behavior and, if examined with the help of a counselor, can be quickly shown to be illogical.

Notice the way in which Vickie brought up the idea that it was time to ask the son to leave. She didn't bluntly say, "I think you should tell him to go," which is blatant advice giving and generally ineffective. Vickie assumed that Edith had already considered it. This is a good tactic because it keeps the counselor from taking on an expert role, and it makes the suggestion seem to be Edith's idea.

If you have read the first eleven chapters in this book, you may have been somewhat surprised at how active the counselor was in this example. This is particularly true in family interventions. Suggestions are more likely to occur in family problems than in individual problems because people often need some new ideas in family problems. They have usually been doing the same things over and over again, not knowing what else to do. Even though you will likely be more active in family counseling, remember that you want to clarify the beliefs first, then draw out the beliefs, the appropriate behaviors, and compare those to the current behaviors.

Now I move to an example of challenging the beliefs when someone obviously holds to a belief that is unhealthy.

BOB. What do you actually believe about parenting?

JAMES. I will always be her dad, and she will always be my daughter.

BOB. That's true enough. I was wondering how much control you think is appropriate for a father to exert over a thirty-one-year-old daughter with two children, who has recently been divorced.

JAMES. She is my responsibility again, and she should do what I tell her.

BOB. How does she feel about your position?

JAMES. I never asked her. I don't ask. I tell.

BOB. Is this the philosophy you used when she was growing up and when she was a teen-ager?

JAMES. You bet it is.

BOB. And with her three brothers when they were teens?

JAMES. Absolutely.

BOB. When was the last time you heard from your two oldest boys?

JAMES. I don't hear from them. They are ungrateful and rebellious. I never hear a word from them.

BOB. Didn't your daughter get pregnant at age seventeen and get married and move out?

JAMES. Yes. I was too easy on her.

BOB. I wonder. It sounds to me like she did what she had to do to get out of the home as fast as possible. Your permanent-parent philosophy does not seem to be producing the kind of happy family results that you would expect from a healthy, accurate philosophy of parenting. Let me ask you a question. Does it sound to you like your approach has worked very well on the first three kids? I might add, isn't the fourth child going to be just as rebellious if he is not given room to grow?

In this example, the parent, James, has been holding on to a rigid, overly controlling philosophy that has driven one child after another out of the house and family. Each time James has blamed the child and never examined himself. This is a somewhat extreme example, but, sadly, it's not as rare as it should be to find such rigid parents.

As you can tell, sometimes a confrontation in counseling can really require the counselor to stick his neck out. I think it's still appropriate to do sometimes, but ideally it should be done after much prayer and thought because if the person doesn't accept your confrontation, you risk losing the friendship. Sometimes love requires you to take such risks, but be sure you examine your own heart first. You probably should never feel good about telling someone else that he is failing. It's usually (but not always) best to wait until you have been given an invitation to express your opinion. Counselors need to be sure they are not guilty of trying to control others. If it hurts you to confront someone, you probably have the right attitude and sensitivity to try it.

Problems with Teens

It seems that every spring a lot of parents drag in their fourteen- or fifteen-year-old children for me to "fix." Frequently the mother has been the primary discipliner, and suddenly the son won't listen to her anymore. There is usually a rather simple explanation. When a boy starts to feel like a man, obeying a woman (his mother) calls him to question and challenge his newfound, fledgling manhood. He feels that obeying her makes him a "boy" and not a "man."

Obeying his father, however, is much simpler. He knows about plenty of examples in which men take orders from other men (army, football), examples in which the manhood of obeying a man is never doubted. Mothers typically snort with disgust at these ideas. Fathers are typically quiet, because they know it's true.

The solution is that dad must pick up the major part of disciplining. Even when he is not there, he needs to leave specific enough instructions so that in his absence the mother can discipline "in dad's name," much as we pray "in Jesus' name." For example, the mother may say to the son who is heading out the door after school, "Remember your dad said to bring in the trash cans and wash the car before you go to play basketball." If the boy disobeys this, he has disobeyed not the mother but the dad. And the dad is the one who will need to do the disciplining.

Several mothers have become very angry at me when I suggested this method, which includes the direction that mother work at retiring from the discipline business with regard to her teen-age son. But almost without exception, they come back and thank me later because they are finally able to relate to the boy. Initially, though, while many moms have been begging dad for just this change, it is difficult for many parents to accept such a change until they see how well it works.

Someone may be asking about a daughter. Is the same switch to father discipline necessary? It seems to be quite necessary in some homes and not in others. It seems to depend on the daughter and also on the mother. In other cases, the dad is so harsh and judgmental that it's best for the mother to handle most of the discipline. Dads tend to be less emotional; in general, therefore, they tend to be less emotional in their discipline methods. If dad is also willing to be responsible and involved, rather than just charge into the middle of a crisis, then his less emotional approach will make him tend to be more consistent. That's a big plus in disciplining.

With somewhat older teen-agers (sixteen to seventeen), parents often take them for counseling (to be "fixed") the first time the teen gets into some significant kind of trouble. Parents often react to that first trouble by wanting to immediately slap a hundred rules onto a child who has had virtually no rules before this. While the hundred-rule response is understandable, it rarely works. Usually, this sudden strictness produces rather significant rebellion.

Avoiding Adolescent Rebellion

Some adolescent pulling away is inevitable, even necessary in a healthy child, but I truly believe that the most extreme cases of antisocial, anti-God, antiparent rebellion can be avoided. First, let's look at the cause of adolescent rebellion. In terms of emotional development, each age has a certain emotional task for the child to accomplish. If it isn't accomplished, it has major implications as to the personality of the child when that child moves into adulthood.

The one thing that an adolescent needs to accomplish on an emotional level is to prove that he's different from mom and dad. He doesn't even need to prove that he is unique just yet (although it is great if he can); he just needs to be different from his parents.

If parents are offended by this (perhaps they are trying to produce clones of themselves rather than independent, unique adults), they will cause one of two things to happen. Either the child will rebel anyway, perhaps more intensely, or the child may never make the transition into adulthood. The child will be emotionally crippled for life and frequently have to ask for extensive professional psychotherapy. The nonrebeller ends up being a really sick adult. In this context, though, I mean pulling away to prove that he is different, not necessarily the ungodly, antisocial behaviors. Pulling away should not be prevented, but I think the antisocial part can be diffused.

Let's remember that the permanent relationship between parents and children is an adult-to-adult relationship. When I talk with parents, they are surprised when I tell them that the child-to-parenting-adult relationship is a temporary one. It lasts only eighteen years. The other relationship of adult-to-adult can last forty years or more. One is designed to end; the other isn't. If a child successfully becomes an adult, then in his parents he can find two friends with many of the same experiences, beliefs, and philosophies he has. Parents can be good friends if they and the children can see themselves as adult friends, not as people with responsibility for one another. True, when the parents become aged, the child may take responsibility for the parents, but that is in the reverse direction of the earlier responsibility. So the adult-to-adult relationship can last for thirty to forty years; on one end the older cares for the younger while on the other end the younger cares for the older. If parents would remember this when their children try to grow up, I think that the parents would fight the end of parenting less.

Freedom within Boundaries

The way to avoid the unhealthy rebellion part of the adolescent's struggle for independence is through the philosophy of parenting called "freedom within boundaries." Ideally, this begins by the time children are eighteen months old. Yes, to avoid trouble at eighteen years, parents should start at eighteen months. Start to do what? Start to train the child for his independence. (Parents should prepare themselves for his independence too.)

Simply put, freedom within boundaries means that the parents establish boundaries of behavior. The child has the freedom of choice within the boundaries and is disciplined consistently if he steps outside the boundaries. The element of choice is vital here because it allows the child to develop an identity that is unique to him. The parents don't fight this, they

171

reinforce it ("Dad likes chocolate, but Billy's favorite is strawberry"). From the years of choosing, the child develops the very same, "I am different from mom and dad" feeling that the rebellion is supposed to produce.

The difficult thing for parents is that the boundaries continually move. If a child is two years old, he may have a hundred rules and limitations. His only element of choice may be what toys to play with or which pajamas he will wear. Even though a child may not understand exactly what it's all about, I would (and I did) take the time to get out two pairs of pajamas and ask the child which one he wants.

At five, the child should have more freedom and responsibility and fewer rules. I would let a five year old pick the cereal he wanted for breakfast, although I wouldn't let him decide whether or not to have breakfast.

At sixteen, if he doesn't want breakfast or pajamas, that's his problem. I would let him take the responsibility for that. The same would be true with many other choices. Ideally, the parents who are trying to work themselves out of a job will regularly say to the child, "We think you are old enough to handle the responsibility of this choice."

By the time the child is seventeen, he should have relatively few rules left. The parents should use what little influence they have left on the really significant issues of life. Length of hair hardly qualifies as a significant issue, and it is a way for a child to express his uniqueness. It is sad to think of how many family nights are ruined by parents trying to exert too much control on their child rather than focusing on training a child for adulthood.

I often wonder if the hundreds of nights of family tension caused by a parent's trying to control his teen's grades in school are really worth it. Who suffers if the child insists on doing no homework or doing homework in a minimally acceptable way? The teen is the one who suffers. Parents are often unwilling for their teens to take the consequences of some bad choices. I understand that, but I wonder how a teen is supposed to learn from his mistakes if he is not given enough freedom to make any. Yes, there are some controls a parent must use and some mistakes a child should be protected from, but probably not nearly as many as most parents would employ. The trick is to combine freedom (choice) with a responsibility. If the child is able to and if a parent is willing for her to handle the responsibility of a certain choice, then she should make that choice and have that freedom and the responsibility.

As you counsel with frustrated parents, remind them that the objective of parenting is supposed to be "letting go," not "controlling." I believe with this simple philosophy, applied consistently, parenting need not be as difficult as it seems for many and it certainly is not as difficult as reacting to one crisis after another with no philosophy at all.

Remarried Reconstituted Families

One of the many new problems this generation must face is that of the reconstituted family. There are often situations with "yours," "mine," and "our" children. Just think of it. It's tough enough to raise children who are blood relatives. What of families with children from three different lines of biological heritage?

It's very difficult to find one guideline or rule to make this situation easy to comprehend. I haven't come up with one yet. Families are so different. Parents are so different. Even individuals change. Sometimes a stepfather relates beautifully to his stepchildren until he and his wife have a child of their own. Overnight the other children are treated like stepchildren.

Added to this is the instability of these situations, with visiting rights, children being gone every other weekend, children moving in every weekend, or children saying, "I want to go live with my father." If anyone believes he understands it, he either needs therapy or needs to write a book.

Its likely, therefore, that you know some people who are struggling to build a stable home in the midst of all this instability. It's also likely you will have the opportunity to lend a listening, caring ear. It's comforting to know that even when there are no easy answers, you can still listen and care.

I suppose the ideal is for both parents to totally accept all children and treat each one the same. Things aren't always that easy, though, and parents who truly love their stepchildren may not be accepted by them. Stepchildren often resent the woman who "replaced" mom or the man who "replaced" dad. If a child is old enough to remember, he may have resentment from the divorce. Even though the new spouse may have had no connection with the divorce and may have come on the scene several years after the divorce, the tendency is to emotionally blame this person for breaking up the family or causing the divorce. The feeling among children is often, *If it wasn't for this person, my mom and dad could get back together.*

Children may silently and unconsciously hold on to the fantasy of the family's getting back together, even after both parents have remarried. To handle this resentment, the parents and stepparents need to remember that they cannot force children to love and accept them. It is far wiser for parents to treat children with understanding, love, and respect than it is to worry about getting them to show loving acceptance. It is immature to think that a child, or anyone, can love only a certain limited number of people. There is no real reason to be threatened by the fact that a stepchild would love the biological parent in a very special way that can never be replaced. Even though there is no reason for it, however, many people do feel threatened. If they realize that there is plenty of love to go around and no one will ever or should ever replace the biological parent, then maybe they can be free to do the job of parenting, which is training the child for adulthood. I advise stepparents (1) to give up trying to replace anybody, (2) to give the child appropriate love, respect, and parenting, and (3) to let the child love them as he will in his own time and in his own way. Parents need to remember the difficult truth that we are there to meet the child's needs, not the other way around.

I said that ideally both parent figures should love each child the same, but we don't really live in an ideal world. Ideally, both parents should work out a plan for discipline and follow that single plan consistently, but sometimes a child will not accept discipline from a stepparent, declaring, "You're not my real mother (father)!" While this hurts, it's also true. Sometimes I advise that the biological parent do the disciplining because it is accepted by the child (in the same way that dad is advised to discipline the teen-age boy simply for the reason that the boy will accept it from him). Conversely, in some cases the stepparent seems to have better parenting instincts, and a child may accept disciplining only from the stepparent rather than from the biological parent.

No government can truly govern without the consent of the governed and families aren't much different. When all else fails, try the pragmatic approach. Do whatever works. I understand that this will be different in different families, but that's really okay. People and families are different.

Too Close Parents

The Bible clearly says that a man shall leave his parents and "cleave" to his wife. This is good advice. It is a shame that more parents don't believe it. Parents often use guilt and other manipulative methods to control or influence their married child's behavior. This is wrong. Parents wouldn't think of treating other adult friends this way, but they do this to adult children without remorse.

My wife loves to say, "Parents give their children two gifts, the first is roots, the second, wings." But, while many parents would agree, some add, "But while you are out flying, be at our house every birthday, holiday, and Sunday dinner."

It's a difficult situation, having to choose between pleasing your parents and your own family. Perhaps this is where the Christian counselor/friend can be helpful. We can help people reexamine their priorities and remember their genuine obligations and responsibilities.

Some time ago a young couple came to me because of the wife's emotional state. She was in constant stress and constantly tearful. Her husband worked as a partner with his dad in a family business, the wife handled almost all the paperwork at the office except some of the bookkeeping the mother retained for herself. The mother continuously criticized, berated, and belittled the wife. In addition, the mother insisted that the couple attend every family function. The husband knew that things were bad, but he was hoping that when dad retired in a few years, he would have the business to himself. Much to this man's credit, when I talked with the couple about the fact that they were too close to his mother, who was not accepting and not treating the daughter-in-law like a daughter or even like a respected adult, the son was ready to do whatever was necessary to protect his wife. I suggested that the couple talk with the husband's parents, setting limits and frankly making certain demands regarding the mother's involvement in the business and her conversation with the daughter-in-law. I told them a little-known secret, which I now tell you. When the children are grown and out on their own with their own lives, their own children, and their own friends, it is the parents who have the greatest need for the relationship with the children. If grown children realize this, they can often use it to win concessions from domineering or demanding parents. They can actually say to the parents, "If you want to see us at all, it will have to be with certain understandings. Without these understandings our family is hurt, and we cannot have that."

The guideline with problems with parents is to put priorities clearly in line in support of wife, husband, and children. Protect your family. Don't let any outside pressure or influence (even from those who reared you) harm your family or deter you from your responsibility to your family. There may be certain responsibilities to others, including parents, but if there is conflict, never sacrifice the primary for the sake of the secondary. If you have to choose between the two, make your priorities clear and the decisions will also be clear.

As a counselor, as you share with people, remember that the counselee may be under tremendous emotional pressure to give in to the parent. Ask him if love really motivates with guilt. I think he will remember that love does not. On the other hand, it is very loving of you to be willing to listen to and care for the pains of your friends.

Because most family problems center around the issue of control, the counselor should guide parents and children toward a healthy set of beliefs about parenting. The model of freedom within boundaries can help prevent the worst of the adolescent rebellion period and will remind parents and children that the goal of parenting is to turn the children into independent adults.

13

Closing Words to Pastors

The counseling ministry can be a powerful way of touching people's lives. And, for a pastor, the one-to-one ministry provides excellent balance to the "one-to-hundreds" of the preaching ministry on Sunday mornings. If the only contact a pastor had with his people was from the pulpit on Sundays, it wouldn't be healthy for either the pastor or the congregation. If preaching is telling, then counseling is listening, caring, and guiding. If you can handle both ends of the spectrum, the telling and the listening/guiding, you have a balance that is both healthy and necessary.

In addition, a pastor needs to see and hear what is happening with his people. He needs to know what they are struggling with and where they are hurting. I doubt if there is a better way to do this than counseling. If the pastor doesn't keep in touch with his people, he loses his ability to understand and to be compassionate, and there is a tendency for his preaching to become more and more harsh and condemning. The preaching of a counseling pastor tends to be more in tune with the people and more understanding and compassionate.

Let's look again briefly at the fruit of the Spirit and see the relevance to the pastoral counselor. "The fruit of the Spirit is love, joy, peace, longsuffering, kindness, goodness, faithfulness, gentleness, self-control" (Gal. 5:22–23). How can we be adequate representatives of the Wonderful Counselor without each of these?

No doubt many people reading this chapter have given numerous sermons on the fruit of the Spirit, so I won't go into great detail, but just to put your mind in the right direction, I want to touch on each fruit briefly and its relevance to counseling.

Love. Some people are easier to love than others, but when counselors don't see the counselee as a loved child of God, we can become judgmental, harsh, and condemning. We can even become insensitive to the pain of the counselee. We need to love, and this needs to be a gift from God of which we are not the source but a channel.

Joy. This doesn't mean giddiness or laughter in front of the suffering of another, but a friendly smile and that inner feeling that life is okay as a servant of the Most High. It is often our inner joy that people see and want. It is often this quality that draws people to seek us out, to find out where that joy comes from. It comes from obeying God, believing Him, and following Him.

Peace. Being a pastor is hardly a peaceful job—being on call twenty-four hours a day, being expected to be all things to all people, being expected to please all factions without being overly aligned with any, being the object of weekly criticism. Even though the job isn't peaceful, if the man in the job is peaceful, he can seem like a shelter amidst the storm. Like Peter walking on the water, he can stay afloat only by keeping his eyes on the Master instead of the waves. In counseling he can show others how to do this. (Of course this is easier if the pastor has some experience in doing it himself.)

Longsuffering. Sometimes a great deal of patience is required to counsel. This is because people change slowly, at their own pace, and also because you may have figured out the problem a long time before you have had the chance to say anything or before the person is ready to hear what you have noticed. You have to wait until the counselee has said what he needs to say, so that he can be ready to hear you.

179

Kindness. What is an act of kindness in counseling? Often it is the willingness to care, to even shed a tear over someone else's pain. A kind man cares about the condition, the experience of those with whom he is counseling.

Goodness. Like the other words on this list, this one has several possible meanings or applications to the pastoral counselor. The one I would like to emphasize is that the counselor must have a purity about him. There can be no place for evil thoughts, impure thoughts, or thoughts that focus on deriving personal gain from information revealed in the counseling or from opportunities the counseling might present.

Faithfulness. At least two meanings come to mind that are relevant to counseling. One is that the counselor needs to be at the appointed place at the appointed time. Take the appointment seriously. The other is that the counselor must be faithful to the counselee. Never break confidences; never talk behind the counselee's back. Your commitment to the counselee is for more than just one hour a week.

Gentleness. This is the opposite of being harsh or blunt. If you are going to say something that is going to hurt someone, you need to be aware of that pain and do your best to cause as little pain as possible. Rarely is the sledgehammer approach really necessary. Christ was usually direct with people, but He was rarely, if ever, harsh.

Self-Control. You need to have your self very much in control to be a good counselor. Physical needs have to be taken care of so that you are not distracted by hunger or the need for sleep. Also, impulses must be controlled. You may have the impulse to tell off one person or to hug another. You need to watch out for both impulses. As much as possible, the counseling is to take care of the counselee's needs, not the pastor's. The pastor's needs and impulses are to be controlled and met at home or somewhere other than in counseling.

Starting Your Counseling Ministry

Some pastors exude such warmth that they hardly ever walk down a hall without hugging at least three people. I have the joy of knowing such a man, and if ever there was such a thing as a visible aura of warmth, he has it. These men don't need to read this section about starting a counseling ministry. They need to read a section on setting limits and saying no. Others, however, don't seem to attract more than the occasional person who comes for counseling.

Here are some suggestions. Ideas in the first chapter, "Getting Started," also can work for pastors. If you really look at people on Sunday, you can often see who needs the attention. Take the initiative and ask when you might get together with these people.

Second, be aware of circumstances in the lives of persons. If someone is going through a difficult time, respond to the circumstance. Make yourself available. Be around the people who are hurting. Invest some time in just being there in their presence, so when they are ready to talk, they will feel as if they know you a little, they will feel as if you care, and they will have the opportunity to talk because of your physical proximity or availability.

Third, use the occasional personal illustration in your sermons. Tell about your own struggle or mistake. In other words, show yourself to be less than perfect. In your own openness people will be more likely to relate to you and share with you. I have often stood in the back of a congregation and watched the congregation's physical reaction when a pastor starts to talk about himself or his family. As soon as he says, "We were struggling with this very thing at home this morning getting ready for church. My daughter said to me..." You can watch the whole congregation sit up and pay attention.

Fourth, without revealing anything in detail, refer in your

sermons to the fact that you do counseling. You might say, "I said to someone in counseling this week that I understood that the Christian life is sometimes difficult and that I was tempted too. You know that person was surprised. He thought he was the only one struggling. Maybe that's because we all come to church and pretend to be perfect. I wonder how we are supposed to grow with an attitude that pretends that we have got it all together?"

When you refer to counseling from time to time, you are accomplishing at least two things. You are letting people know that you consider counseling to be an important part of your ministry, thereby planting the idea that you might be someone to talk to. And by the stories you tell, you are giving them at least a general idea about how you respond in counseling.

Conflicts with Confidences

Sometimes a situation will come up when you feel that something you know from counseling should affect some other decision outside the counseling. You might know that a man is a secret problem drinker, and you might be present when he is being nominated for deacon or elder. Or you may have been counseling with a man who is having an affair, trying to get himself free from that emotional bondage. Then, when his wife comes in for counseling and says that her husband is acting strangely and she doesn't know what to do, you may be tempted to reveal a confidence.

In a board meeting or nominating committee meeting, I hope that the pastor would have enough credibility with the board to be able to say something like, "This is not a good time for Bob right now. We have talked some, and I think he would want us to wait on that nomination."

Whenever possible, the counselee should be allowed or encouraged to make his own revelations. Different churches operate differently, of course, but some pastors would just not say anything in the board meeting and let the man do his own declining. Depending on the circumstances, that can be a perfectly acceptable procedure.

The problem with the wife's asking the pastor about what is wrong with her husband is harder to handle. The pastor has no right to tell the wife what he knows from private counseling with her husband. If he told her, he could even be sued. I was once working with a couple, seeing them both separately, when the husband said, "As of this moment you are no longer doing marriage counseling. You are doing divorce counseling. I have a girlfriend and I have decided to divorce my wife, but I am not going to file that suit for several months. You may not tell my wife." I went through some very difficult, frustrating months, but I did not break his confidence because I had no right to.

There is a more difficult situation that arises, and that is when someone in an official or public ministry in the church is involved in a secret sin, perhaps sexual in nature, for which he is coming to you for counseling. I suggest that you ask the counselee to take some action on his own with regard to his position. He need not reveal the details. He need only take the action with as general an explanation as he wishes. If he refuses, then you have a conflict between your pastoral role and your counselor role. You might warn him that you have a conflict and ask his help, or you might possibly let him know that if he does not handle the problem himself within a certain period of time, you will feel compelled to do something. You might injure the counseling relationship by doing this, but there may be no alternative in some cases.

How Much Counseling Should You Do?

Obviously there are many different churches with many different needs. There are also different pastors with different styles of ministry. I cannot presume to use one formula for everyone. However, I do know that there is a limit to how much counseling one person can handle. With experience, tolerance increases, but with too much counseling in a given week, you run the genuine risk of burn-out. At some point then, it becomes poor stewardship of your time and overall ministry to see so many people in counseling that your effectiveness as a pastor decreases.

When I was doing private practice in psychotherapy and nothing else, I put a limit of thirty-two hours a week on the practice. I found that with more than that, it took me too many days to recover my emotional equilibrium. I would end up feeling drained, tired, and even "down" emotionally.

With the many responsibilities of a pastor, I think it would be rare for a pastor to be able to adequately handle more than twelve to fifteen one-hour sessions a week. This doesn't mean that you should feel guilty if you only have time or emotional energy for five or six sessions. I am only suggesting that twelve or fifteen is probably the upper limit.

Another issue is how many sessions a pastor should see one particular person. In a church of five hundred people, is it really good stewardship to see the same six people over and over, month after month, if by so doing the pastor cannot see other members of the body who also need help? If this is sometimes a problem, here is one thought to consider. Some pastors of large churches limit the number of sessions they will see someone for counseling. If the person still needs help after a certain number of sessions (four, six, or eight), then the pastor will refer the person to an associate, a Christian counselor, a counselor on the church staff, or a member of the church's lay counseling team (see the following section). If this is a consistent policy for everyone, then it can be applied without its appearing to be favoritism or prejudice. I think that limiting the number of sessions a pastor of a large church would see any person for ongoing counseling makes sense.

Lay Counseling Team

This book has been designed to help not just full-time Christian workers but also Christian men and women in the church. If it is true that pastors are to equip men and women to do the work of the ministry, then consider teaching a team of men and women in your church the basic counseling tools in this book. (You might want to contact the publisher of this book and ask about a series of videotape training sessions taught by this author.)

In addition to the training courses in counseling, I strongly urge you to set up an ongoing lay counselor support group in your church, led by either yourself or someone else with some training and experience in counseling. This group could meet every week or two. In addition to some brief input to the group and/or a review of an article or a book, the counselors could talk about their problems, share suggestions, make prayer requests, and pray. Any ministry that is going to last needs ongoing attention. Don't just start it up and let it go. By investing one to two hours a week in this equipping ministry, the pastor greatly multiplies his own effectiveness.

"Teaming" with Your Wife

Some pastors' wives are intimately involved in the church ministry. Others are not. Some pastors and their wives work well together, others do not. But in general, if a pastor and his wife can counsel together, they can increase their effectiveness.

Many pastors, families, and churches have been so badly damaged by counseling relationships getting out of hand that the wise pastor will do everything possible to protect himself, his family, and his parishioners. I have dealt with this earlier by telling laymen flatly that no men should counsel women by themselves or vice versa. As a pastor, you may not have the same luxury of simply saying no to someone for counseling. But you can include your wife.

Some pastors' wives develop an excellent ministry of counseling, and the pastor simply refers a woman to his wife. While that is great, sometimes it can be even more effective for the pastor and his wife to counsel as a team. This can be done in individual therapy or perhaps with a couple in marriage counseling.

In some cases the pastor still does the lion's share of the active counseling, and the wife listens, prays, observes, and makes an occasional comment. In other couples, both people have specific skills and both participate. If both are going to be active, it's a good idea to talk together before each session about what you are working on and what you are trying to achieve.

In marriage counseling, the couple approach can be particularly effective. Each person of the couple coming for counseling can have an advocate, as it were, and no one feels "ganged up on." It is really true that two heads are better than one, and with practice and openness on both sides, the sum of the two is often greater than either could have been separately. Of course, the counseling couple also acts as a model for communication and cooperation.

Pastors as Counselors

As I have implied, preaching is usually seen as a pastor's number one duty. It is often the prophetic or "telling forth" the truths of God that they feel called to when they become pastors. However, this may differ significantly from the priestly role of confessor and reconciler.

As a pastor gets used to being the authority figure, the administrator, the leader, the one who tells, it can become more and more difficult for him to suddenly shift gears and listen. On the other hand, if the pastor remembers his shepherd role, the man with a caring, pastor's heart will be a natural for a counseling ministry. A pastor's heart, his dependence on God, and his training and skills make the picture complete.

14

Closing Words to Pastors' Wives

As you already know if you are a pastor's wife, many congregations expect the pastor's wife to be a feminized version of the pastor. They expect leadership skills, teaching skills, and counseling skills. These are added to the more traditional "wifely" skills of being sociable, hospitable, loving, caring, and so forth.

Whether or not the congregation expects you as a pastor's wife to have an active counseling ministry, they do expect you to know how. Most congregations think that the pastor's wife has some special training to be a pastor's wife. It doesn't occur to most parishioners (and they don't take the time to analyze their expectations) that the pastor marries a person who may or may not have special training. If a pastor marries a real estate person, an insurance underwriter, or a criminologist, the congregation still typically expects his wife to perform in the feminized pastor role. More than perhaps any other job, the pastor's wife is often considered when the pastor is going through the interviewing "calling" process.

Does a pastor's wife who is led to a ministry of counseling do that counseling any differently from anyone else? Probably not. The basic skills would be the same as those already addressed in the rest of this book.

I felt the need to direct a few pages to pastors' wives because I believe they may have one of the most difficult jobs in the world. It is all the more difficult because the congregation's expectations of her (in other words, her job description) vary so widely from church to church and even from family to family within the church.

In Church X, most people may expect the pastor's wife to have an active counseling ministry. This is often based on the previous pastor's wife. Or if the previous pastor's wife was unpopular, their expectations may come from the wife of the pastor before that.

I hope this book has given you some basic guidelines on what to do when you are in a counseling role. In addition to these general guidelines, there are a few specific counseling situations that you can expect to come in contact with, even if you don't pursue a counseling ministry. These are situations that will be thrust upon you simply because you are the pastor's wife.

Phone Counseling

As I was doing the research for this chapter, most pastors' wives mentioned a recurring situation. People often call their house in an emergency or crisis, hoping to talk to the pastor but not finding the pastor in. After saying that he is not in, it is usually a good idea for the pastor's wife to ask, "Is there anything I can do to help?" Often, people simply need to tell someone what's going on. They may just need to talk for a while, and your role is clearly to listen.

I suggest active listening kinds of skills that we discussed earlier. Respond verbally with "uh huh," "oh my," "I see." Also, use the understanding and caring techniques we examined in earlier chapters. Tell the person what you think he is feeling, "That sounds awful," "You must have been terrified," "I'm sure that hurt." Sometimes tell the person what you are feeling about what he is saying, "I can see why you would be upset," "I am so sorry that happened." Of course you generally only say what you are feeling if you are feeling something positive. If you are feeling something negative, it's better not to share that in the crisis counseling situation. Usually that would be done only in the context of an ongoing personal or counseling relationship.

I know you don't need my permission, but I encourage you to put a reasonable time limit on these crisis phone calls. I usually listen for five to ten minutes and that's about it. After ten minutes you have had a chance to hear, one time through, just about any problem. You can often tell that the caller is feeling calmer after a few minutes. The easiest way to terminate the phone call is to talk about your husband's response or ask what the caller wants you to tell your husband.

You might say, "I expect my husband home between 10:00 and 11:00 tonight. I will tell him that you called. Will you need for him to call you tonight, or would you rather just call him at the office in the morning?" You will often find that after their telling you, they feel well enough to wait until morning. Also, I would suggest that you not commit your husband to calling when he gets home. It is probably better to say, "I will tell him that you called and that you would like to hear from him" rather than, "I will have him call you tonight when he gets in." Obviously, this is a general guideline. I wouldn't presume to tell you how you and your husband should work out the details of your own communication.

Crisis: A Time for Advice

As you know by now, I am not too thrilled about counselors giving much advice in most kinds of counseling. Crisis phone counseling, however, is one notable exception. At the end of many crisis phone calls, I will try to find three specific things for the caller to do when he hangs up. This is specifically so that he can feel more in control and so that he can take his mind off the crisis for the night. If a person has gotten himself worked up enough to make a crisis phone call, the chances are very good that he has already spent hours focusing on the problem without benefit.

The counselor's objective in the crisis phone call is not so much solving the problem as it is getting the person through the night, so that he can work on his problem solving when things are a bit calmer and his mind is clearer. Feel free to be creative in what you suggest here. What you suggest is not nearly so important as the fact that you are suggesting something. I will often have the person make a glass of warm milk to drink (it has surprising tranquilizing properties), and I may suggest that he put on a record of calm praise music and perhaps read some Psalms. Other ideas include making a note to call someone for an appointment tomorrow (my personal favorite), making a list of things to do tomorrow and, of course, trying to get some rest.

I will often end a crisis phone call with prayer. It is a good thing to do because it directs the caller's mind toward a loving God so that he doesn't have to feel so alone. It helps the counselor's feeling of helplessness, and it helps end the phone conversation. Because you don't always know the caller, often it's a good idea to ask if you can pray for him. I usually say, "Would it be all right if I prayed for you right now, before we hang up?" Afterward you can just say, "Okay then, Bill, be sure to call in the morning for an appointment. Good night."

Confidentiality

Perhaps an additional word about confidentiality is appropriate in this chapter. Pastors' wives are often privy to confidential information about people. Even though, as a rule, the pastor's wife is not usually someone who will reveal a confidence, and it goes without saying that this is important, it is also important not to accidentally reveal what you know.

Frankly, it is hard to remember where you heard everything and whether something is general knowledge or privileged information. Most times, if a confidence is revealed by a pastor's wife, it will be done accidentally. All I want to do is to remind you to think about what you are saying before you say it and try to ask yourself where that information came from. This is good advice for anyone.

When you are with people from the church who have been in counseling with your husband, they will often assume that you know all about what they said in counseling, and that may be true. But frequently you won't even know that they were in counseling, let alone what they were talking about. It is probably best in both situations to speak and act as though you know nothing. This way, if the people want you to know, they can tell you themselves. Quite often what you do know isn't what they think you know anyway.

What should you do if you know something that, if the pastor knew, would affect somebody's situation in the church or the pastor's decision in church? In other words, how do you keep the confidences of your own counseling from your husband, the pastor? This is a difficult situation. I don't have any easy answer. In general it is good to encourage your counselee to tell the pastor himself if it's something the pastor should know. You might even share that your knowing what you know puts you in a difficult position, and ask the counselee to tell the pastor or ask for permission to talk with your husband about it.

Working with Your Husband

There will be times when you will accompany your husband on a pastoral visit to a house or perhaps a hospital visit. I recommend that you explicitly ask your husband what he expects from you. If you don't know, all you can do is assume, and that causes trouble far too often for it to be a good idea. No matter what you believe about equality or submission, if you are going along on a pastoral visit, it is part of his job so he is to set the limits.

If your husband stopped in to see you at your place of employment, how would you want him to act? You would hope and expect that he would respect your wishes regarding how he acts where you work. I think you are in a similar situation when you participate in the church ministry as the wife of a pastor.

Is It Okay to Be Yourself?

I know I have just opened the lid on a real can of worms. The problem? You are attending church at your husband's place of employment. This is your primary source of friends, support, and aggravation. How free are you to be yourself? How free should you be? I don't know the answer. I am not sure if there is one right answer, but I don't think there is. My guess is that the right pastor's wife role is the one that is right for you.

I know some women who say clearly, "I was not called to the ministry, my husband was. I was called to be his support—a wife, friend, and mother to our children." These women sometimes refuse traditional pastor's wife jobs in the church, and they keep a very low profile in the church. They don't automatically attend the church every time the doors are open. They might even say, "That's his job, not mine."

Some readers will be offended or even shocked by this approach. It is clearly not for everyone, but I frankly support it as one legitimate way for some women who are married to pastors to stay sane. These women are criticized, of course, but I doubt that they are criticized any more than the active pastor's wife and possibly less. I believe that some criticism simply comes with the territory. If you are going to be criticized anyway, you might as well do what you think is right for you and your family and get criticized for that rather than violate yourself to please others and still get criticized.

Other pastors' wives are very active and involved. They feel as called to the ministry as their husbands and often refer to their team ministry. This is just as appropriate as another model, if it is who you genuinely are and what you genuinely believe God has called you to do and to be.

Often, how close you work with your husband may have as much to do with his style as it does with yours. You can still be involved, even if it is not closely with your husband, if you want to be. Find an area of interest that your husband is not heavily involved with and enter it wholeheartedly. Feel free to carve out your own niche.

Oh yes, you'll get criticism for being active. It might be for being too loud, too quiet, or too pushy. It might be for not conforming to traditional expectations or for almost anything. I hope you will remember to do a little self-counseling when this happens. Perhaps you can ask yourself, "Who owns this problem?" If you start out realizing that 10 percent of the church will disapprove no matter what you do or how you do it, then you might be a bit freer to make your own decisions based on what is going to please you and God. And whether it's counseling you decide to do, or music, Christian education, commercial art, or real estate, you can be who God designed you to be without slavery to fear.

15

Closing Words to Lay Counselors

As campus workers, such as people from Campus Crusade or InterVarsity Christian Fellowship discovered long ago, there is a wide open door into the hearts, minds, and souls of people if you will listen to them, care about them, and become their friend. There are occasions for going up to people and telling them about God, but most adults who give their lives to the Lord have been brought to Him by a friend.

I enjoy listening to people give their testimonies about how and when they first came to know Jesus personally. If you listen to these testimonies, looking for the influence of godly friends, you will find it in probably 90 percent of the cases.

People often say, "I can't go up to a total stranger and ask him, 'Do you know God?' " I won't debate that issue here, but I do want to point out that friendship ministry is something that everyone can do.

I remember asking a dear elderly Christian saint about her non-Christian friends and being surprised because she was offended. "I have no non-Christian friends" was her reply. I wonder how we can have an impact on our world if we never talk to that world and don't know anybody who doesn't believe the same way we do.

In recent years it seems to me that the Christian church has become affected by a kind of Hollywood-star mentality, with highly visible, highly paid professionals who perform and the rest of us who watch. This is not what a body is all about. In a body, every cell has its own function.

Some people reading this have been longing for a ministry they can do. Some cannot teach or sing, aren't comfortable in leadership positions, and perhaps feel like second-class Christians and only "affiliate members" of their churches. I want to encourage you to take up the challenge of ministry to people, whether they are believers or nonbelievers. Minister to them one at a time. How do you do that? Listen to them, care about their needs, be their friend. This is a ministry you can do because Jesus is the Wonderful Counselor and you are just the local representative. On top of that, as a believer, you have been given the Holy Spirit who Christ himself called "the Helper." If you ask Him, He will certainly help you.

Sword Practice

Most of us know that we are to have daily devotions to keep in tune and in touch with God. While this is certainly true, that is only part of the reason we are to study the Word. The Bible is called the sword of the Spirit. It is the Christian's only offensive weapon. Our faith is a shield, a defense against the attacks of the enemy. While stopping the fiery darts is vital to survival, wielding the sword is the one thing that actually drives the enemy away. *Star Wars* introduced the light saber into our awareness. It is, in essence, a sword of light. As I understand it, there could be no more accurate description of the Bible than as a sword of light. As believers, we can use it to drive away the enemy. We can't use our own words against Satan because they would be useless, but God's words are sharp, powerful rays of light that dispel Satan's darkness.

Yet, as Christians, if we never do battle, we forget what the sword is for. Our sword is not just for elaborate exhibitions or for ceremonies. Our sword is for battle. One reason our devotions, and indeed our whole Christian life, may seem bland or dull from time to time is the lack of battle.

But a believer doing battle with the darkness of pain, fear, discouragement, and bondage can remind you of that battle. What I am saying is this. Another good reason to get involved with counseling is that, properly perceived, it forces you to exercise faith (thereby strengthening your faith) and wield your sword (thereby giving you reason to practice and making your Bible study alive).

Faith is involved just in sticking your neck out and saying, "You look unhappy. How are things?" to somebody. You need faith to say, "Let's get together. I want to support you during this time." And you need faith while you are counseling to seek God's guidance and filling. You need faith to open your mouth, faith to keep it closed, and faith to know how to fill it. Obviously the combination of a sword of light and a shield of faith is a powerful combination, or God would not have given it to us in our Christian armor.

Prayer

I hope you will pray every day for your counseling ministry. I hope you will take it seriously. Prayer will include the people that you are currently seeing and the people that God wants to use you to help tomorrow or next week. Specifically ask God to lead you each day to the people that you can help with a word of care or comfort or a listening ear. I know that God wants us all to be loving people, so if you will ask for His guidance and power to do His will, you will receive what you ask.

Also pray for others in the counseling ministry. (I would appreciate it if you would pray for me.) Pray for the training and support group that you need in your counseling ministry as well as the Christian professional you need for guidance or to whom you can refer people. I have prayed for everyone reading this paragraph that God will lay someone on your heart, even now, He wants to use you to care for, listen to, or understand.

Responsibility

A word of reminder. When someone tells you of a problem, ask yourself, *Who owns this problem?* If it is not your problem, don't carry it. Care about it, but don't carry it. I think the only times I have gotten into trouble as a counselor are times when I have taken on the responsibility to fix someone else's problems rather than help them fix the problem themselves.

If the person you are counseling is going on and on about someone else's problem, notice that right away. Your job will not be to fix that problem, but to get your counselee to see that he cannot fix someone else. He must be responsible for his own attitude and behaviors. Almost everyone who worries about someone else's problem is avoiding taking responsibility for his own.

I think that every believer can be and is to be the lighthouse on his own block, the signpost pointing the way to Jesus. The Bible says that we, as Christians, will help Jesus rule during the millennium. Each of us can work on those "ambassador" skills now by representing Christ to a hurting world. I close with a prayer I try to pray every day. Originally it was known as the prayer of Saint Francis of Assisi. I suggest that another title might be "The Counselor's Prayer":

Closing Words to Lay Counselors

Lord, make me an instrument of thy peace.
  Where there is hatred, let me sow love;
  Where there is injury, pardon;
  Where there is doubt, faith;
  Where there is despair, hope;
  Where there is darkness, light, and
  Where there is sadness, joy.
Oh Divine Master, grant that I may not so much seek to
    be consoled, as to console;
To be understood as to understand;
To be loved as to love.
For it is in giving that we receive;
It is in pardoning that we are pardoned;
It is in dying that we are born to eternal life.

Appendix

The Taylor-Johnson Temperament Analysis (T-JTA)* is an easily administered and easily scored paper and pencil test designed to show personality traits. Its popularity comes in part from its easily understandable profile, which can be shown directly to the counselee.

The test is also popular because of the crisscross feature that allows husbands to describe their wives and wives their husbands. Robert M. Taylor, president of Psychological Publications, Inc., has graciously given permission for me to include these sample profiles in *Called to Counsel*.

The self descriptions on the sample profiles are indicated with solid lines labeled HUSBAND or WIFE. Crisscross answers (descriptions or ratings of one by the other) are indicated with broken lines labeled HUSBAND BY WIFE or WIFE BY HUSBAND.

As you look at Sample Profiles 1 and 2, you will see that the first describes the husband and the second the wife.

In Sample Profile 3, both the husband's and the wife's profiles are plotted together.

Sample Profiles 4 and 5 add the spouse's description to the self description.

Taylor-Johnson Temperament Analysis (T-JTA), Taylor, Robert M., and Morrison, Lucile Phillips, by Psychological Publications, Inc., 5300 Hollywood Blvd., Los Angeles, CA 90027. 1966–1985.

Sample Profile 4 gives you the husband's description of himself (solid line, repeated from the first sample) and adds his wife's description of him (broken line).

And on Sample Profile 5, you have the wife's description of herself (solid line, repeated from the second sample profile) along with her husband's description of her (broken line).

You can readily see the wealth of material the premarital counselor or the marriage counselor can derive from these tests. For example, if the tests show two very dominant people, or perhaps one overly dominant spouse and one extremely passive spouse, there is much fruit for discussion.

The text is published and can be obtained from Psychological Publications, Inc., 5300 Hollywood Boulevard, Los Angeles, California 90027 (213-465-4163). Please understand that, as with all psychological tests, the T-JTA is available only to people with a professional degree from a college or seminary, with appropriate course background in psychology, counseling, and so forth. Please address your questions regarding the test directly to them.

HUSBAND   SAMPLE PROFILE 1

TAYLOR-JOHNSON TEMPERAMENT ANALYSIS PROFILE
Profile Revision of 1967

Name_____WHITE, ROBERT P._____ Age 39 Sex M Date 6-27-68

School U of CALIF Grade 14 Degree_____ Major BUS. ADM. Occupation SALESMAN_____ Counselor R.T.

Single_____ Years Married 18 Years Divorced_____ Years Widowed_____ Children: M 1 Ages 16 F_____ Ages_____

Answers made by: SELF and/or husband, wife, father, mother, son, daughter, brother, sister, or_____ of the person described.

Norm(s):1947-8 Gen. Pop.	A	B	C	D	E	F	G	H	I	Attitude (Sten) Score: 7
Mids		1			2	3	1	2	1	Total Mids: 10
Raw score	10	3	36	32	28	17	35	28	33	Raw score
Percentile	50	27	91	65	28	81	95	96	84	Percentile
TRAIT	Nervous	Depressive	Active-Social	Expressive-Responsive	Sympathetic	Subjective	Dominant	Hostile	Self-disciplined	TRAIT

HUSBAND

TRAIT OPPOSITE	Composed	Light-hearted	Quiet	Inhibited	Indifferent	Objective	Submissive	Tolerant	Impulsive	TRAIT OPPOSITE

Excellent   Acceptable   Improvement desirable   Improvement urgent

DEFINITIONS

TRAITS

Nervous – Tense, high-strung, apprehensive.
Depressive – Pessimistic, discouraged, dejected.
Active-Social – Energetic, enthusiastic, socially involved.
Expressive-Responsive – Spontaneous, affectionate, demonstrative.
Sympathetic – Kind, understanding, compassionate.
Subjective – Emotional, illogical, self-absorbed.
Dominant – Confident, assertive, competitive.
Hostile – Critical, argumentative, punitive.
Self-disciplined – Controlled, methodical, persevering.

OPPOSITES

Composed – Calm, relaxed, tranquil.
Light-hearted – Happy, cheerful, optimistic.
Quiet – Socially inactive, lethargic, withdrawn.
Inhibited – Restrained, unresponsive, repressed.
Indifferent – Unsympathetic, insensitive, unfeeling.
Objective – Fair-minded, reasonable, logical.
Submissive – Passive, compliant, dependent.
Tolerant – Accepting, patient, humane.
Impulsive – Uncontrolled, disorganized, changeable.

Note: Important decisions should not be made on the basis of this profile without confirmation of these results by other means.

Printed by permission of Psychological Publications, Inc.

WIFE   SAMPLE PROFILE 2

TAYLOR-JOHNSON TEMPERAMENT ANALYSIS PROFILE
Profile Revision of 1967

Name _____ WHITE, JOAN _____ Age 37 __ Sex F __ Date 6-27-68

School COMPLETED Grade 12 Degree ____ Major ____ Occupation HOUSEWIFE ____ Counselor R.T.

Single ____ Years Married 18 Years Divorced ____ Years Widowed ____ Children: M 1 Ages 16 F ____ Ages ____

Answers made by: SELF and/or husband, wife, father, mother, son, daughter, brother, sister, or _____ of the person described.

Norm(s)1967-B GEN. POP.	A	B	C	D	E	F	G	H	I	Attitude (Sten) Score: 4
Mids	1	1	1		1	1	1			Total Mids: 6
Raw score	15	9	17	26	37	11	13	4	28	Raw score
Percentile	62	46	14	25	78	51	16	24	61	Percentile
TRAIT	Nervous	Depressive	Active-Social	Expressive-Responsive	Sympathetic	Subjective	Dominant	Hostile	Self-disciplined	TRAIT

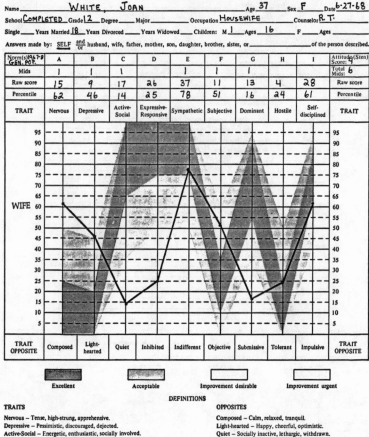

| TRAIT OPPOSITE | Composed | Light-hearted | Quiet | Inhibited | Indifferent | Objective | Submissive | Tolerant | Impulsive | TRAIT OPPOSITE |

Excellent   Acceptable   Improvement desirable   Improvement urgent

DEFINITIONS

TRAITS

Nervous – Tense, high-strung, apprehensive.
Depressive – Pessimistic, discouraged, dejected.
Active-Social – Energetic, enthusiastic, socially involved.
Expressive-Responsive – Spontaneous, affectionate, demonstrative.
Sympathetic – Kind, understanding, compassionate.
Subjective – Emotional, illogical, self-absorbed.
Dominant – Confident, assertive, competitive.
Hostile – Critical, argumentative, punitive.
Self-disciplined – Controlled, methodical, persevering.

OPPOSITES

Composed – Calm, relaxed, tranquil.
Light-hearted – Happy, cheerful, optimistic.
Quiet – Socially inactive, lethargic, withdrawn.
Inhibited – Restrained, unresponsive, repressed.
Indifferent – Unsympathetic, insensitive, unfeeling.
Objective – Fair-minded, reasonable, logical.
Submissive – Passive, compliant, dependent.
Tolerant – Accepting, patient, humane.
Impulsive – Uncontrolled, disorganized, changeable.

Note: Important decisions should not be made on the basis of this profile without confirmation of these results by other means.

Printed by permission of Psychological Publications, Inc.

COUPLE

SAMPLE PROFILE 3

HUSBAND AND WIFE
TAYLOR-JOHNSON TEMPERAMENT ANALYSIS PROFILE
Profile Revision of 1967

Name WHITE, ROBERT P., AND WHITE, JOAN Age 39 37 Sex M F Date 6-27-68

School U. OF CALIF. COMM. Grade 14 12 Degree _____ Major BUS. ADM. Occupation SALESMAN HOUSEWIFE Counselor R.T.

Single _____ Years Married 18 Years Divorced _____ Years Widowed _____ Children: M 1 Ages 16 F _____ Ages _____

Answers made by: SELF and/or husband, wife, father, mother, son, daughter, brother, sister, or _____ of the person described.

Norm(s): M67-67 Gr.P. Gr.P.	A		B		C		D		E		F		G		H		I		Attitude (Sten) Score: 7 7
Mids		1	1		1		1		2	1	3	1	1	1	2		1		Total Mids: 10 6
Raw score	10	15	3	9	36	17	32	26	28	37	17	11	35	13	28	4	33	28	Raw score
Percentile	50	62	27	46	91	14	65	25	28	78	81	51	95	16	96	24	84	61	Percentile
TRAIT	Nervous		Depressive		Active-Social		Expressive-Responsive		Sympathetic		Subjective		Dominant		Hostile		Self-disciplined		TRAIT

| TRAIT OPPOSITE | Composed | Light-hearted | Quiet | Inhibited | Indifferent | Objective | Submissive | Tolerant | Impulsive | TRAIT OPPOSITE |

Excellent — Acceptable — Improvement desirable — Improvement urgent

DEFINITIONS

TRAITS

Nervous – Tense, high-strung, apprehensive.
Depressive – Pessimistic, discouraged, dejected.
Active-Social – Energetic, enthusiastic, socially involved.
Expressive-Responsive – Spontaneous, affectionate, demonstrative.
Sympathetic – Kind, understanding, compassionate.
Subjective – Emotional, illogical, self-absorbed.
Dominant – Confident, assertive, competitive.
Hostile – Critical, argumentative, punitive.
Self-disciplined – Controlled, methodical, persevering.

OPPOSITES

Composed – Calm, relaxed, tranquil.
Light-hearted – Happy, cheerful, optimistic.
Quiet – Socially inactive, lethargic, withdrawn.
Inhibited – Restrained, unresponsive, repressed.
Indifferent – Unsympathetic, insensitive, unfeeling.
Objective – Fair-minded, reasonable, logical.
Submissive – Passive, compliant, dependent.
Tolerant – Accepting, patient, humane.
Impulsive – Uncontrolled, disorganized, changeable.

Note: Important decisions should not be made on the basis of this profile without confirmation of these results by other means.

Printed by permission of Psychological Publications, Inc.

HUSBAND BY WIFE SAMPLE PROFILE 4

CRISS—CROSS

TAYLOR-JOHNSON TEMPERAMENT ANALYSIS PROFILE

Profile Revision of 1967

Name WHITE, ROBERT P. Age 39 Sex M Date 6-27-68

School U. OF CALIF. Grade 14 Degree ____ Major BUS. ADM. Occupation SALESMAN Counselor R.T.

Single ____ Years Married 18 Years Divorced ____ Years Widowed ____ Children: M 1 Ages 16 F ____ Ages ____

Answers made by: SELF (and) or husband, wife, father, mother, son, daughter, brother, sister, or ____ of the person described.

Norm(s): 1967-8 G.P. C.C.	A	B	C	D	E	F	G	H	I	Attitude (Sten) Score: 7 4
Mids		1	1		2 1	3 2	1 2	2 2	1	Total Mids: 10 8
Raw score	10 16	3 8	36 37	32 28	28 9	17 28	35 38	28 38	33 26	Raw score
Percentile	50 59	27 39	91 94	65 49	28 6	81 92	95 99	96 99	84 56	Percentile
TRAIT	Nervous	Depressive	Active-Social	Expressive-Responsive	Sympathetic	Subjective	Dominant	Hostile	Self-disciplined	TRAIT

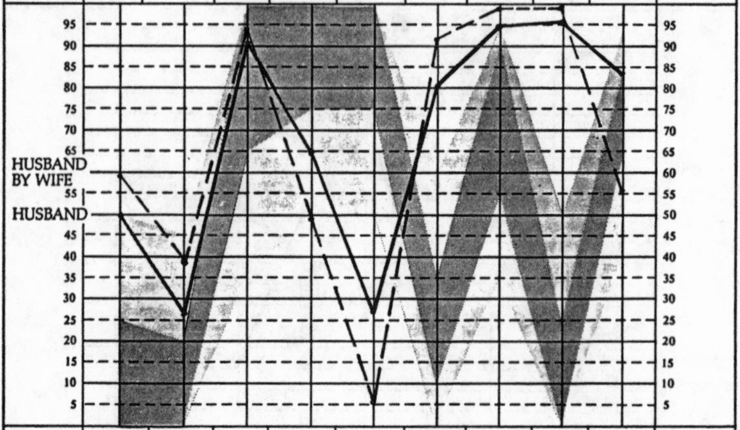

95
90
85
80
75
70
65
HUSBAND BY WIFE
60
55
HUSBAND
50
45
40
35
30
25
20
15
10
5

TRAIT OPPOSITE	Composed	Light-hearted	Quiet	Inhibited	Indifferent	Objective	Submissive	Tolerant	Impulsive	TRAIT OPPOSITE

Excellent
Acceptable
Improvement desirable
Improvement urgent

DEFINITIONS

TRAITS

Nervous – Tense, high-strung, apprehensive.
Depressive – Pessimistic, discouraged, dejected.
Active-Social – Energetic, enthusiastic, socially involved.
Expressive-Responsive – Spontaneous, affectionate, demonstrative.
Sympathetic – Kind, understanding, compassionate.
Subjective – Emotional, illogical, self-absorbed.
Dominant – Confident, assertive, competitive.
Hostile – Critical, argumentative, punitive.
Self-disciplined – Controlled, methodical, persevering.

OPPOSITES

Composed – Calm, relaxed, tranquil.
Light-hearted – Happy, cheerful, optimistic.
Quiet – Socially inactive, lethargic, withdrawn.
Inhibited – Restrained, unresponsive, repressed.
Indifferent – Unsympathetic, insensitive, unfeeling.
Objective – Fair-minded, reasonable, logical.
Submissive – Passive, compliant, dependent.
Tolerant – Accepting, patient, humane.
Impulsive – Uncontrolled, disorganized, changeable.

Note: Important decisions should not be made on the basis of this profile without confirmation of these results by other means.

Printed by permission of Psychological Publications, Inc.

WIFE BY HUSBAND

SAMPLE PROFILE 5

CRISS-CROSS

TAYLOR-JOHNSON TEMPERAMENT ANALYSIS PROFILE
Profile Revision of 1967

Name_____WHITE, JOAN_____Age_37_Sex_F_Date 6-27-68

School COMPLETED Grade 12 Degree_____ Major_____ Occupation HOUSEWIFE_____ Counselor R.T.

Single____ Years Married 18 Years Divorced____ Years Widowed____ Children: M 1 Ages 16 F____ Ages_____

Answers made by: SELF and husband, wife, father, mother, son, daughter, brother, sister, or_____ of the person described.

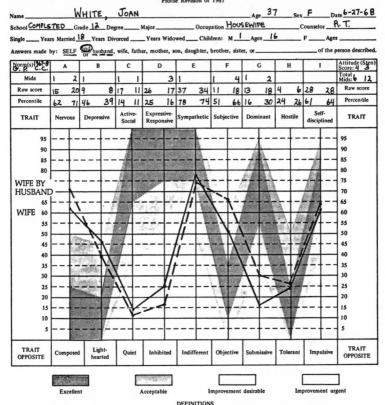

Norm(s) 36T-8 Q. P. C.C.	A		B		C		D		E		F		G		H		I		Attitude (Sten) Score: 4 3
Mids	1	2	1		1	1		3	1		4	1	1	2					Total Mids: 6 12
Raw score	15	20	9		8	17	11	26	17	37	34	11		18	13	18	4	6	28	28	Raw score
Percentile	62	71	46	39	14	11	25	16	78	74	51	66	16		30	24	26	61	64	Percentile
TRAIT	Nervous		Depressive		Active-Social		Expressive-Responsive		Sympathetic		Subjective		Dominant		Hostile		Self-disciplined		TRAIT

| TRAIT OPPOSITE | Composed | Light-hearted | Quiet | Inhibited | Indifferent | Objective | Submissive | Tolerant | Impulsive | TRAIT OPPOSITE |

Excellent   Acceptable   Improvement desirable   Improvement urgent

DEFINITIONS

TRAITS

Nervous – Tense, high-strung, apprehensive.
Depressive – Pessimistic, discouraged, dejected.
Active-Social – Energetic, enthusiastic, socially involved.
Expressive-Responsive – Spontaneous, affectionate, demonstrative.
Sympathetic – Kind, understanding, compassionate.
Subjective – Emotional, illogical, self-absorbed.
Dominant – Confident, assertive, competitive.
Hostile – Critical, argumentative, punitive.
Self-disciplined – Controlled, methodical, persevering.

OPPOSITES

Composed – Calm, relaxed, tranquil.
Light-hearted – Happy, cheerful, optimistic.
Quiet – Socially inactive, lethargic, withdrawn.
Inhibited – Restrained, unresponsive, repressed.
Indifferent – Unsympathetic, insensitive, unfeeling.
Objective – Fair-minded, reasonable, logical.
Submissive – Passive, compliant, dependent.
Tolerant – Accepting, patient, humane.
Impulsive – Uncontrolled, disorganized, changeable.

Note: Important decisions should not be made on the basis of this profile without confirmation of these results by other means.

Printed by permission of Psychological Publications, Inc.

7